# Introduction

Literacy is the key that unlocks all learning. Very young children can be introduced to literacy in a fun, playful way by using finger plays, flannelboard stories, and puppets. The assortment of rhymes, poems, and literature selections provided in this series are research based and classroom tested. A variety of suggestions are presented to guarantee the use of standards-based curriculum to assist young learners in exploring basic concepts.

This book is one of three in a series that will introduce educators to ideas for enhancing language experiences, exploring creativity and imagination, and teaching children to enjoy literacy. The materials were compiled to support teachers who may be pressured by the emphasis in education arenas to teach using standards-based criteria and the challenge of how to implement standards-based curriculum in a practical fashion in the classroom.

The Language Arts, Mathematics, and Science Standards for Early Childhood addressed in each section are listed in the beginning of the unit. One or more teaching tips to support the use of the materials accompanies each unit, as does an art activity for expansion of the concept. Ideas for supporting children with special needs, additional enrichment activities, and suggested books round out each unit of stories and patterns.

The activities included in this series are developmentally appropriate practices that support the whole child. The materials presented allow for kinesthetic (tactile), auditory, vocal, and visual stimulation. The mastery of oral language is a prerequisite to effective emergent literacy. Children learn about the relationship between spoken and written language as they hear, tell, and retell stories. They begin to understand how to create a story sequence with a beginning, a middle, and an end. Children orally practice behaviors that will later be critical to learning to read (the link between pictures and words) and to write (the ability to say it, sequence it, and show it in print).

The suggested flannelboard stories and puppets are enticing visual and tactile aids that make learning a hands-on experience. By watching and then manipulating the puppets, children will solidify concepts while improving their motor skills. Puppets allow the young child a safe place to experience the world of imagination. Sometimes a shy child will speak to a puppet before speaking to an adult. Positive self-esteem is strengthened when children have the opportunity to successfully manipulate the puppet and say the story themselves. The initial time spent creating these materials is well worth the effort, not to mention the fun! The patterns are versatile and can be used in different stories.

In *Puppet & Flannelboard Stories for Seasons and Holidays,* children are introduced to many basic concepts through the exploration of a variety of literature selections. The flannelboard stories, rhymes, and finger plays are presented in four thematic units. Each unit is based on a season—fall, winter, spring, and summer. The contents will assist the students with basic phonemic awareness and auditory discrimination and can be used to provide an introduction to phonics. The selected stories are favorites. Be creative and add your own seasonal and holiday ideas.

Simple, easy-to-make puppets and related activities accompany each presentation. Young learners are introduced to seasons and holidays by memorizing the different pieces of selected literature and acting them out with a teacher. Mathematics and literacy skills are developed along the way. Later, the youngsters can reinforce what they have learned by using the puppets to retell the stories amongst themselves.

The standards for Language Arts, Mathematics, and Science listed on pages 4, 5, and 6 are met with the activities in *Puppets & Flannelboard Stories for Seasons and Holidays*. These compilations of standards and objectives are similar to the ones required by your school district. The pages can be posted in the classroom for reference when planning lessons and for parent information. Family members are often surprised at the amount of "learning" inherent in storytelling.

Every attempt has been made to give credit to authors of individual stories, though many have been passed down through oral tradition. We apologize for any original sources we are unable to identify.

# Standards for Language Arts

- ❏ Listens
- ❏ Comprehends what others are saying
- ❏ Asks and answers questions
- ❏ Demonstrates competency in speaking
- ❏ Demonstrates competency in listening
- ❏ Is developing fine motor skills
- ❏ Follows simple directions
- ❏ Identifies and sorts common shape words into basic categories
- ❏ Identifies characters, settings, and important events
- ❏ Produces meaningful linguistic sounds
- ❏ Produces rhyming words in response to an oral prompt
- ❏ Recites familiar stories and rhymes with patterns
- ❏ Recites short stories
- ❏ Recognizes colors
- ❏ Recognizes color words
- ❏ Recognizes meaningful words
- ❏ Responds to oral directions
- ❏ Responds to oral questions
- ❏ Retells familiar stories
- ❏ Auditorily tracks each word in a sentence
- ❏ Understands that printed material provides information
- ❏ Uses picture clues to aid comprehension
- ❏ Uses picture clues to make predictions about content

The standards above are a compilation from the National Association for the Education of Young Children, the National English Language Standards for Public Schools, and the National Standards for English Language Arts.

# Standards for Mathematics

- ❑ Conceptualizes one-to-one correspondence
- ❑ Compares whole numbers
- ❑ Connects math with the real world
- ❑ Connects math with other disciplines
- ❑ Copies and extends patterns
- ❑ Counts to ten
- ❑ Describes basic shapes
- ❑ Divides objects into categories
- ❑ Estimates quantities
- ❑ Explores activities involving chance
- ❑ Identifies equal/unequal portions
- ❑ Identifies shapes in the real world
- ❑ Identifies shapes in different positions
- ❑ Implements a problem-solving strategy
- ❑ Learns number names
- ❑ Makes predictions
- ❑ Names basic shapes
- ❑ Recognizes and collects data
- ❑ Solves simple equations
- ❑ Sorts basic shapes
- ❑ Uses verbal communication
- ❑ Uses pictorial communication
- ❑ Uses symbolic communication
- ❑ Understands the problem
- ❑ Classifies objects

The standards above are a compilation from the National Association for the Education of Young Children, the National Standards for English Language Arts, and the National Council for Teachers of Mathematics.

# Standards for Science

☐ Applies problem-solving skills

☐ Classifies

☐ Communicates

☐ Discusses changes in seasons

☐ Explores animals

☐ Explores fish

☐ Explores insects

☐ Identifies the five senses

☐ Identifies objects by color

☐ Identifies objects by properties

☐ Identifies objects by shape

☐ Identifies objects by size

☐ Identifies color in the real world

☐ Observes, identifies, and measures objects

☐ Observes and identifies objects

☐ Predicts

☐ Problem solves through group activities

☐ Recognizes opposites

The standards above are a compilation from the National Association for the Education of Young Children and the National Science Foundation (NSF).

# The ABC's of Storytelling

**A**dapt the story for your group. Shorten, expand, or change the wording for different age levels. The attention span of young children can vary tremendously.

**B**e creative with ways to enhance involvement and promote active participation. For example, ask everyone to clap when they hear a certain word.

**C**heck for understanding, monitor and adjust learning as you watch, and listen to your students. Use children's names and tell children what they did. For example, "That is correct, Juan. You knew it was a blue square."

**D**evote time to preparation. Make certain you know the story and have all the follow-up materials ready. Accentuate the plot and characters.

**E**mphasize the incidents that appeal to children. For example, the element of surprise can create vehicles for application in the real world. Use real-life examples and pictures when available.

**F**requently ask children to respond. Ask them to repeat a line or give you a similar word. Plan ways to reinforce basic language principles.

**G**ain children's attention prior to beginning the story. For example, sing a favorite song everyday. The consistency and structure will help remind the children that it is time for storytime.

**H**old the book so that the children can see, or point to, the figures on the flannelboard.

**I**ndividualize your instruction. Think about each child in your group and choose stories that align with his or her likes and interests.

**J**ustify literacy! Send home notes to parents letting them know the book, story, or poem you are teaching. Ask them for support at home. Encourage parents to reread the story at home for reinforcement.

**K**nowledge of the early childhood standards will enhance your teaching. Review the charts provided in this book and integrate these standards into your lesson plans.

**L**ist the key concepts for a story, and repeat the learning throughout storytime. Make lesson planning a valuable component of your program. Keep the key learning lists and plan to spiral back to them to reinforce concepts.

**M**aterials should be age appropriate. Use the teaching tips and expansion activities for children with special needs or those in need of enrichment.

# The ABC's of Storytelling *(cont.)*

**N**ew books are wonderful, but the old favorites are just as grand! Use a variety of titles in your classroom.

**O**pen, body, close should be the sequence of every storytime. Open with an attention-getter. Preview the activity, follow with the body of the story, and close with some type of review or follow-up activity.

**P**acing is critical. Check yourself during the lesson; "Am I moving too quickly, too slowly?" If the children are restless, change the pace or try a different activity.

**Q**uestion the children. Ask focused questions like, "What else works like this?" Ask the children to repeat/retell the story. Ask, "How do you think the story will end?" Ask, "Do you know what will happen next?" Use eye contact and affirm the children's answers.

**R**epeat favorites; children learn through repetition. Reread or retell the story many, many times.

**S**it in close proximity, at the level of the children whenever possible. Providing a set structure for circle time supports learning. Sit in the same place; always begin with a familiar opening transition song, etc.

**T**reasure teachable moments. If a child wants to relate the story to his or her own life (maybe he or she has the same breed of animal as in the story), allow the time, and use it as a teachable opportunity.

**U**tilize all available space, both in the area you are telling the story and on the flannelboard (if using a flannelboard).

**V**ary your facial expression and use your voice as a tool. You may want to whisper to emphasize a special part of the story.

**W**ords you use should be clear and simple. Enunciate and speak slowly.

**X**-ray vision—Use eye contact as an antecedent to prevent unacceptable behavior.

**Y**our attitude is contagious! If you have fun and enjoy storytime, so will the children with whom you work.

**Z**ZZZZZZZZZZ-end. Emphasize the end of the story and draw closure to the lesson with follow-up and/or extension activities. This will help children remember the story and concepts covered. When they arrive home and a parent asks, "What did you learn in school today?", they are more likely to recall the story and concepts learned if there has been closure to the lesson.

# Creating Flannelboards

There are many flannelboards on the market; however, sometimes creating your own is more appealing. You know what size and shape your classroom can accommodate. Cut a large piece of corrugated cardboard to the size you wish to create a flannelboard. Cut a piece of felt 1" (2.54 cm) larger than the cardboard. Cover the cardboard with the felt, and tape or glue the overlap in the back. (Note: Light blue makes a good background, since sky is often a good backdrop. A black background, on the other hand, can be quite striking.) Consider the following ideas when designing your own flannelboard.

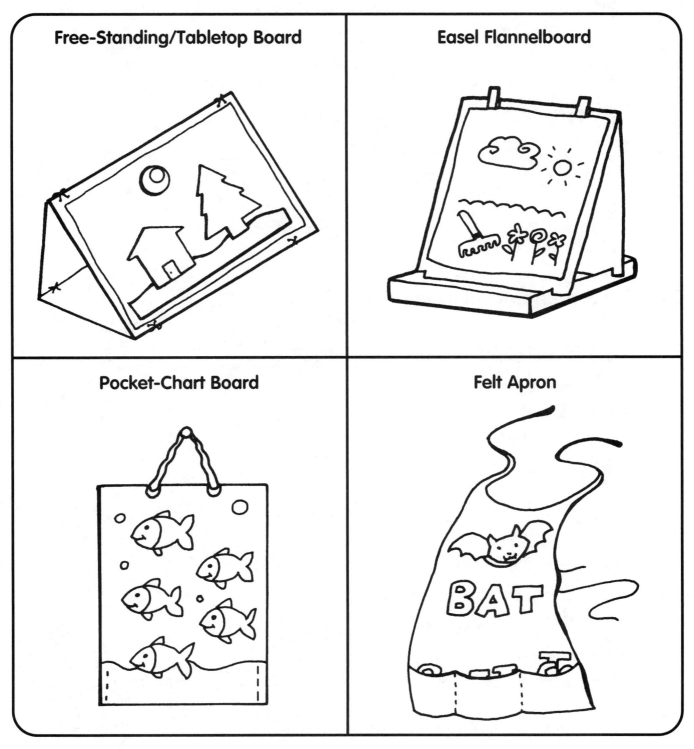

**Free-Standing/Tabletop Board**

**Easel Flannelboard**

**Pocket-Chart Board**

**Felt Apron**

BAT

# Creating Flannelboard Characters

Flannelboard characters are inexpensive to make and provide wonderful visuals for young learners. The patterns provided in this book can be made with felt or other materials and assembled with standard glue or a glue gun. Some require simple sewing. All patterns can be enhanced with decorations. Use your imagination. Incorporate your own ideas and those of the children to construct personalized teaching tools for your own classroom.

Cut the original patterns out of heavy cardstock or cardboard and laminate them. These patterns should be saved in a central file area or in the same container as the figures and the story. This way, if one is lost or ruined, it is simple to replace.

## Tips for Enhancing Flannelboard Pieces

1. Use scissors with different edges when cutting out paper pieces to be attached to felt backing. Many styles are sold in craft, hobby, and fabric stores. Some have rounded edges, some are scalloped, and some have zigzag edges. Pinking shears are fun, too, and they work on fabric!

2. Keep leftover scraps of felt and fabric from other projects. You never know when a small piece will come in handy as a decoration, an eye, or a clothing detail.

3. Collect scraps of ribbon, bows, trim, and buttons.

4. Use leftover glitter and sequins for special details. Glitter glue and puff paints are handy as well. Consider using them when creating royal characters or when adding scales to a fish.

5. Yarn and curling ribbon make great hair.

6. Attach a small piece of Velcro® or felt to the back of most small puppets for use on the flannelboard.

7. Cut out characters from old storybooks and magazines. Attach them to felt with glue. Use these just as you would a felt piece.

# Additional Uses for Patterns

The patterns included in this book are quite versatile and simple to use. The more you work with them, the more uses you will discover for them.

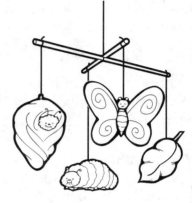

- Reproduce the patterns on construction paper, and provide the children with materials to color, cut out, and glue the pieces together. Then they can have a set of figures for each story to take home and practice with parents or other family members.

- Use the patterns to create story mobiles and hang them from the ceiling.

- Magnetic strips can be glued to the backs of some flannel pieces for use on a magnetic board.

- Use the patterns as placeholders on the classroom calendar.

- Use the patterns to create an individual big book as a keepsake for each child in the class. For each book, cut two pieces of poster board to the desired size. Glue the pattern and copy of the story onto each of the pages. Be sure to make an extra book for your reading corner or reading station!

- Children love to tell and retell stories. Consider making a second set of patterns for each story. The duplicate pieces can be kept in the children's story area. Allow children to mix and match the pieces to create new stories, or to retell variations of the favorites you have shared with them.

## Additional Resources

Gould, Patti and Joyce Sullivan. *The Inclusive Early Childhood Classroom: Easy Ways to Adapt Learning Centers for ALL Children.* Gryphon House Publishers, 1999.

This book offers a variety of excellent strategies designed to adapt curriculum centers for children with special needs.

Sandall, Susan and Ilene Schwartz. *Building Blocks for Teaching Preschoolers with Special Needs.* Paul H. Brooks Publishing Company, 2002.

The authors provide many creative ideas for curriculum modifications, teaching and embedding learning opportunities, and child-focused instructional strategies.

## Puppets and Flannelboard Sets

**Artfelt,** 1102 N. Brand Blvd., San Fernando, CA 91340 (818) 365-1021. E-mail: artfelt@mail.com

Artfelt offers a wide selection of products. Their quality finger and hand puppets are designed to also work on felt boards, bulletin boards, and pocket charts.

# Creating Puppets

There are many materials you can use to create puppets. Below you will find five different types of puppets and directions for their creation. Some will incorporate the patterns supplied in this book, and others can be made easily with household or classroom items.

## Stick Puppets

Patterns for stick puppets can be copied onto heavy cardstock or cardboard, cut out, and decorated. Some teachers like to laminate the pieces. The cutouts can then be attached to craft sticks, tongue depressors, paint stirrers, or yardsticks for easy accessibility.

Mini stick puppets can be made by attaching stickers to craft sticks.

Don't forget about wooden spoons. Faces can be drawn or glued onto them to create almost instant puppets.

**Note:** When telling the story, whoever is designated to hold the puppet holds onto the item (type of stick) to which the pattern was attached.

## Pop-Up Puppets

The element of surprise is a valuable attention-getting device in the early childhood classroom. Use a cylinder (paper tube), coffee can, Styrofoam cup, or paper cup for the base of the pop-up puppets.

Poke a hole in the center and insert a craft stick, sturdy straw, or dowel. Attach an old doll head (or a head created from a Styrofoam ball wrapped with yarn or covered with nylons) to the dowel.

Use a glue gun to attach the head to the dowel if the dowel cannot be pushed into the head. For added interest, decorate the handmade head with yarn, fabric, etc.

# Creating Puppets *(cont.)*

## Hand Puppets

Use old gloves to create puppets for the number stories. Attach a small strip of Velcro® with a glue gun to each finger of the glove. Use the glove puppet when introducing Three Little Pumpkins, Five Little Ghosts, or another counting story. Put one finger puppet on each glove finger.

There are many other objects that can be used for hand puppets. If you take some of the stuffing out of a stuffed animal, you will have a wonderful puppet. It is best to remove the stuffing from a slit in the back or the bottom of the animal. Leave the head, arms, and/or legs filled.

Mittens, paper bags, feather dusters, socks, a Slinky®, shirt sleeves, rubber gloves, and kitchen hot pads can all be used to create hand puppets. Use a variety of materials to create the face(s) of the character(s) in the story you are telling.

## Face Puppets

A face puppet can be created on a paper plate, dust pan, sponge, Ping-Pong paddle, fly swatter, paintbrush, or wooden spoon. Decorate the face to match the characters or animals in the corresponding story.

## Finger Puppets

Simple, one-time-only, finger puppets can be made by covering a child's fingertips with masking tape or stickers. Faces can be drawn on the tape or plain stickers. Seasonal stickers, such as pumpkins, can also be used for specific stories or songs.

To make a more permanent puppet, glue felt pieces or pictures to a film canister or cut off the fingers of old gloves and decorate them with a permanent marker or felt details.

Finger puppets can also be made by cutting out two small, identical pattern pieces and gluing them together, leaving a small opening at the base of a finger to fit it. Any puppet small enough to fit on a glove will work for a finger puppet.

# Ideas for Storage

There are many ways to store puppets and felt pieces. Try to keep all of the characters for one story in the same container. Always include a copy of the story. This organizational method can come in handy for people who do not memorize the stories and need the written words or prompts. Consider adding a list of the required props on the container. This is especially useful when some of the props used are from other stories or are materials used in other areas of the classroom.

Storage options include the following ideas:

Tape a file folder together on two sides and staple string to the top for a handle. Attach the story or write its title on the outside of the folder. List the props on the other side of the folder.

**The Turkey**

Label a gallon-size, plastic resealable bag with the title of the story. Enclose a copy of the story and the puppet pieces. Consider attaching a three-ring strip to each bag. The felt figures and the corresponding stories can then be stored in a large three-ring binder for easy access.

Collect new pizza boxes (many shops will gladly donate them to schools). Attach the story to the lid and place the pieces inside. If you plan to stack these boxes, it is a good idea to label the side of the box as well.

Popcorn

Create a storage container out of a shoebox. Add a copy of the story. Laminate it if possible. List the contents of the box on the inside of the top of the lid.

# Fall Unit

A variety of holidays and celebrations provide opportunities for oral language, expansion of vocabulary, and concrete reinforcement of visual learning. Fall is a season for changes. The leaves change colors; the plants are harvested. The weather is getting colder. Provide the children with experiences such as walking in piles of leaves. Encourage them to draw pictures and to tell stories about these activities. Write the stories down. Have the children share their stories at group time.

## Teaching Tips

Bring a basket of apples to group time. Hold an apple in one hand. Ask the children if they know what is inside an apple. Reinforce oral language skills by allowing each child an opportunity to guess what he or she believes is inside. After everyone has had a chance to make a prediction, cut the apple horizontally across the middle. Show the children the star that is inside. Cut an apple for each child and allow him or her to create his or her own story about the star. At the end of the activity, let the children eat the apples for a snack.

With the harvest season celebrations and the Thanksgiving holiday, fall is an appropriate time to talk about extended families and to hold a feast. Invite parents and extended family members to share a special noon meal with the children. Each family is asked to bring a favorite dish from his or her culture to share. The children learn about a variety of cultural traditions and have an opportunity to sample different dishes.

Grind corn using a matate (mortar and pestle). Talk about how difficult it is to do. Tell the children that a long time ago people had to grind corn, but that today we purchase cornmeal at the store. Make cornbread for a snack.

## Art Activities

Create a paper-bag turkey. Allow each child to use crayons to color the top half of a lunch bag. Stuff the bag half full with shredded newspaper. Close the top of the bag with a rubber band. Make the head and feet out of construction paper using the patterns on page 38.

Create a turkey from an apple. Use raisins for the eyes and gumdrops on toothpicks for the feathers. Attach a small piece of licorice for the mouth.

## Supporting Children with Special Needs

A group project is a wonderful way to include children with special needs. Have a variety of paints available in fall colors. Allow each child to dip one hand into the paint and create a hand print. After the prints have dried, cut around them creating "leaves" for the tree. Children can cut pictures of things for which they are thankful out of old magazines and hang them on the trunk. The resulting bulletin board will display all your students' fantastic fall artwork.

## Enrichment

Share the poem to the right with the children. After you have read it through twice, encourage them to think of other words they could add to the poem relating to each season.

| Seasons |
| --- |
| Fall is wheezy, sneezy, freezy. |
| Winter is slippy, drippy, nippy. |
| Spring is showery, flowery, bowery. |
| Summer is hoppy, croppy, poppy. |

## Book Suggestions

Barner, Bob. *Dem Bones.* Chronicle Books, 1996.

Ehlert, Lois. *Red Leaf, Yellow Leaf.* Harcourt Children's Books, 1991.

King, Elizabeth. *The Pumpkin Patch.* Puffin Books, 1996.

# Meeting the Standards: Fall Unit

## Language Arts

- Listens
- Comprehends what others are saying
- Asks and answers questions
- Demonstrates competency in speaking as a tool for learning
- Demonstrates competency in listening as a tool for learning
- Is developing fine motor skills
- Follows simple directions
- Produces meaningful linguistic sounds
- Produces rhyming words in response to an oral prompt
- Recites familiar stories and rhymes with patterns
- Recites short stories
- Recognizes colors
- Recognizes color words
- Responds to oral directions
- Responds to oral questions
- Retells familiar stories

## Mathematics

- Conceptualizes one-to-one correspondence
- Divides objects into categories
- Connects math with the real world
- Connects math with other disciplines
- Copies and extends patterns
- Counts to ten
- Identifies shapes in the real world
- Identifies shapes in different positions
- Implements a problem-solving strategy
- Learns number names
- Makes predictions
- Uses verbal communication
- Uses pictorial communication
- Uses symbolic communication

## Science

- Applies problem-solving skills
- Classifies
- Communicates
- Discusses changes in seasons
- Identifies the five senses
- Identifies objects by color

- Identifies objects by properties
- Identifies objects by shape
- Identifies objects by size
- Identifies color in the real world
- Observes, identifies, and measures objects

# School Is Starting

It is September.  Fall is here.

It is my favorite time of year.

September means I go to school.

And I learn finger plays that are really cool.

At school we tell stories that are so much fun.

There is a lot to learn for everyone.

**Teacher Suggestion:** Use this page as a letter to parents introducing the stories and finger plays you will be sharing with the children during the school year.  Share the poem with the students and have them color the page before taking it home.

# Leaf Poem

## Like a leaf or a feather, in the windy, windy weather,

*(Hold the leaves high above your head and move them back and forth.)*

## We will whirl around, and twirl around,

*(Stand up and turn around with the leaves still in your hands.)*

## And all fall down together.

*(Let the leaves drop down to the floor.)*

**leaf patterns**

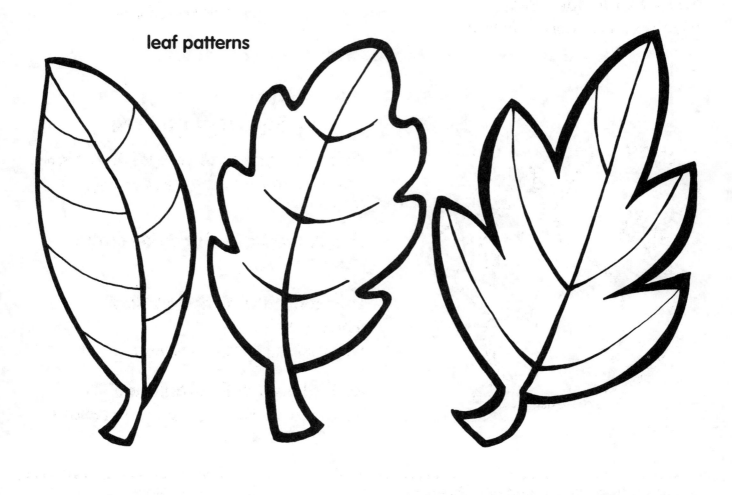

• • • • • • • • • • • • • • • • • • • • • • • • • • • • • • • • • • • • • • • • • • •

Use the patterns above to make several different fall-colored leaves.

• • • • • • • • • • • • • • • • • • • • • • • • • • • • • • • • • • • • • • • • • • •

# Chipmunk and Squirrel Poems

## Striped Chipmunk

**A little striped chipmunk**
**Sat up in a tree,**
*(Make a fist and protrude your thumb.)*

**Counting all his chestnuts,**
**One, two, and three.**
*(Point to three fingers.)*

**When little Betty Boston went out**
**to play, the chipmunk flipped**
**his tail,**
**And ran far, far away!**
*(Hide one hand behind your back.)*

## Squirrel in a Tree

**This is a squirrel that lives in a tree;**
*(Place the squirrel and the tree on the flannelboard.)*

**This is the tree which he climbs.**
*(Point to the tree.)*

**This is the nut that he takes**
**from me**
*(Place the nut on the flannelboard.)*

**As I sit very still sometimes.**
*(Place your hands in your lap and sit quietly.)*

1. Make one squirrel and one chipmunk.
2. Use the patterns here and on page 20 to accompany, or in place of, the hand motions given above.

# Patterns for Squirrel in a Tree

nut

tree

1. Make one tree.
2. Make one nut.

# Pumpkin Poems

## Five Little Pumpkins

**Five little pumpkins standing in a row.**
*(Have five children stand in a line.)*

**Three stood straight and two bent low.**
*(Have three children stand up tall and two bend over.)*

**Along came a skeleton and what do you think?**
*(The teacher can be the skeleton or you can use the skeleton pattern on page 23.)*

**Up jumped those pumpkins, quick as a wink.**
*(Have the children jump up quickly.)*

## Five Little Jack-O'-Lanterns

**Five little jack-o'-lanterns sitting on the fence.**
*(Place five jack-o'-lanterns on the flannelboard.)*

**One said, "Good-bye, things are getting tense."**
*(Take one jack-o'-lantern off the flannelboard.)*

**Four little jack-o'-lanterns feeling very wary.**
**Another one left, he said things were too scary.**
*(Take one jack-o'-lantern off the flannelboard.)*

**Three little jack-o'-lanterns with lights shining bright.**
**One thought he'd roam on Halloween night.**
*(Take one jack-o'-lantern off the flannelboard.)*

**Two little jack-o'-lanterns looking very brave.**
**"See you next year," one said with a wave.**
*(Take one jack-o'-lantern off the flannelboard.)*

**One little jack-o'-lantern waiting to be seen.**
*(Place the black cat on the flannelboard.)*

**Left with a black cat who'd come out on Halloween.**
*(Take the last jack-o'-lantern and the cat off the flannelboard.)*

• • • • • • • • • • • • • • • • • • • • • • • • • • • • • • • • • • • • • •

Use the patterns on pages 22-23 to create the skeleton, five jack-o'-lanterns, and black cat flannel pieces.

• • • • • • • • • • • • • • • • • • • • • • • • • • • • • • • • • • • • • •

# Patterns for Pumpkin Poems

**five  pumpkins**

Use the patterns above with the poems on page 21 and the patterns on page 23.

# Patterns for Pumpkin Poems *(cont.)*

skeleton

black cat

1. Make one skeleton for "Five Little Pumpkins."
2. Make one black cat for "Five Little Jack-O'-Lanterns."

# House with the Door

## Knock on the door.

*(Put the house with the door on the flannelboard. Make a knocking motion.)*

## Say, "Trick or treat."

*(Have the children say, "Trick or treat.")*

## Open the door.

*(Open the door of the house.)*

## Whom do we meet?

**Teacher Suggestion:** Create a variety of characters using flannel pieces from the different flannelboard stories in this book. (For example, you could use a witch, a ghost, etc.) Reinforce language development and vocabulary expansion by asking the children to tell you whom they meet as the door opens.

Use the patterns on page 25 to create the house and door flannel pieces.

# Patterns for House with the Door

**door**

**house**

1. Make the house out of heavy tagboard.
2. Attach the door so that it will open. Use a brad for the doorknob.

# Owl Poems

## The Funny Little Owl

There's a funny little owl, in a funny little tree.
*(Hold up the owl puppet.)*

Singing, "Whooo woo, whooo woo, you can't scare me."
There's another little owl, in another little tree.
*(Use your other hand to hold up the second owl puppet.)*

Singing, "Whooo woo, whooo woo, you wait and see."
**Boo!**

## The Owl and the Wind

Oh, did you hear the wind last night,
A-blowing right at you?
It sounded just as though it said,
"Ooooooo-Ooooooo-Ooooooo!"
*(Encourage the children to make
the ooooo sound.)*

The wind now has a playmate
Just as most children do.
He sits up in a tree and hoots,
*(Hold up the owl.)*

"To-whooo, to-whit, to-whooo."
*(Encourage the children to say
the words with you.)*

So when you hear the owl
  and the wind
Just at the close of day,
They're calling to each other
To come out now and play.

Use the pattern on page 27 to create the owl puppet.

# Pattern for Owl Poems

**owl**

1. Make and decorate two owls for "The Funny Little Owl." Cut two holes where the beak should be.
2. Insert your thumb and forefinger in the holes to manipulate the owl puppet.
3. Make one owl for "The Owl and the Wind" following the directions above.

# This Is Halloween

One little skeleton hopping up and down,
*(Put the skeleton on the flannelboard.)*
Hopping up and down, hopping up and down.
One little skeleton hopping up and down, for this is Halloween.

Two little witches flying through the air,
*(Place two witches on the flannelboard.)*
Flying through the air, flying through the air.
Two little witches flying through the air, for this is Halloween.

Three little pumpkins walking in a row,
*(Place three pumpkins on the flannelboard.)*
Walking in a row, walking in a row.
Three little pumpkins walking in a row, for this is Halloween.

Four little jack-o'-lanterns skipping down the street,
*(Add a fourth pumpkin and the faces to create four jack-o'-lanterns.)*
Skipping down the street, skipping down the street.
Four little jack-o'-lanterns skipping down the street, for this is Halloween.

Five spooky spiders hanging from a web,
*(Put five spiders on the flannelboard.)*
Hanging from a web, hanging from a web.
Five spooky spiders hanging from a web, for this is Halloween.

Six black cats prowling in the night,
*(Place six cats on the flannelboard.)*
Prowling in the night, prowling in the night.
Six black cats prowling in the night, for this is Halloween.

Seven little owls sitting in the tree,
*(Add seven owls to the flannelboard.)*
Sitting in the tree, sitting in the tree.
Seven little owls sitting in the tree, for this is Halloween.

Eight black bats hanging upside down,
*(Place eight bats on the flannelboard;
be sure they are hanging upside down!)*
Hanging upside down, hanging upside down.
Eight black bats hanging upside down, for this is Halloween.

Nine little children playing trick or treat,
*(Line up nine children to play trick or treat.)*
Playing trick or treat, playing trick or treat.
Nine little children playing trick or treat.
For this is Halloween!

# Patterns for This Is Halloween

witch

girl

boy

. . . . . . . . . . . . . . . . . . . . . . . . . . . . . . . . . . . . . . . . . . . . . . . . . . . . . . . .

**Teacher Suggestion:** Use the patterns on pages 22, 23, 29, 30, and 34 to create several stick puppets representing the characters in this poem. Allow each child to select a stick puppet, and stand up and hold the puppet during the appropriate stanza.

Follow the directions on the next page to make a counting flannelboard story.

. . . . . . . . . . . . . . . . . . . . . . . . . . . . . . . . . . . . . . . . . . . . . . . . . . . . . . . .

# Patterns for This Is Halloween *(cont.)*

spider

owl

bat

. . . . . . . . . . . . . . . . . . . . . . . . . . . . . . . . . . . . . . . . . . . . . . . . . . . . . . . . . . . . . . . . . .

1. Make one skeleton using the pattern on page 23.
2. Make two witches using the pattern on page 29.
3. Make three pumpkins using the patterns on page 34.
4. Make four jack-o'-lanterns using the patterns on page 22.
5. Make five spiders.
6. Make six black cats using the pattern on page 23.
7. Make seven owls.
8. Make eight bats.

. . . . . . . . . . . . . . . . . . . . . . . . . . . . . . . . . . . . . . . . . . . . . . . . . . . . . . . . . . . . . . . . . .

# Five Little Ghosts

**Five little ghosts on Halloween night.**

*(Have five children stand up.  Give each one a ghost stick puppet to hold.)*

**One was so tired he slept through the night.**

*(Have one child sit down.)*

**Four little ghosts flying so high.**

**One was so scared he started to cry.**

*(Have another child sit down.)*

**Three little ghosts as happy as can be.**

**One flew so high he bumped into a tree.**

*(Have another child sit down.)*

**Two little ghosts dancing in the air.**

**One did the hokey-pokey; he didn't care.**

*(Have another child sit down.)*

**One little ghost all alone in the night.**

**He said, "Boo," and gave himself a fright.**

*(Have the remaining child sit down.)*

Use the patterns on page 32 to create a variety of ghost stick puppets.

# Patterns for Five Little Ghosts

**five ghosts**

1. Enlarge the ghost patterns if possible.
2. Attach each ghost to a craft stick.

# Halloween Song

*(Sing to the tune of "Are You Sleeping?")*

## Here is a pumpkin.

*(Place the tall, oval pumpkin on the flannelboard.)*

## Here is a pumpkin.

*(Place the round, fat pumpkin on the flannelboard.)*

## Halloween, Halloween.
## Tall and oval,
## Round and fat.

*(Point to the pumpkins as you describe them.)*

## Turn them into jack-o'-lanterns
## Just like that!

*(Flip over the pumpkins to show the jack-o'-lanterns.)*

## Jack-o'-lantern,
## Jack-o'-lantern
## Halloween, Halloween.
## See the witches flying.

*(Place the witches on broomsticks
on the flannelboard.)*

## Hear the wind a-crying
## Ooooo-ooooo-ooooo, Ooooo-ooooo-ooooo.

*(Encourage the children to say the sounds along with you.)*

• • • • • • • • • • • • • • • • • • • • • • • • • • • • • • • • • • • • • • • • • • •

Use the patterns on page 34 to create the pumpkins, jack-o'-lanterns, and broomstick flannel pieces.

• • • • • • • • • • • • • • • • • • • • • • • • • • • • • • • • • • • • • • • • • • •

# Patterns for Halloween Song

round, fat pumpkin

tall, oval pumpkin

facial features for pumpkins

. . . . . . . . . . . . . . . . . . . . . . . . . . . . . . . . . . . . . . . .

1. Make one tall oval-shaped pumpkin.
2. Make one round fat pumpkin.
3. Add facial features (yellow) to the back of each pumpkin.
4. Make several witches or broomsticks using the pattern on page 29.

. . . . . . . . . . . . . . . . . . . . . . . . . . . . . . . . . . . . . . . .

# Three Blind Bats

*(Sing to the tune of "Three Blind Mice.")*

## Three blind bats, three blind bats.

*(Place three blind standing bats on the flannelboard.)*

## See how they fly, see how they fly.

*(Place three flying bats on the flannelboard in place of the standing bats.)*

## They fly with witches and birds so high.

*(Place the witches, birds, and ghosts on the flannelboard.)*

## They scare the ghosts right out of the sky.

*(Pull the ghosts off the flannelboard.)*

## Did you ever see such a Halloween sight
## As three blind bats?
## Three blind bats.

Use the patterns on page 36 to create the standing bats, birds, witches, and ghosts flannel pieces. Use the three bats above to create flying bats.

# Patterns for Three Blind Bats

bat

bird

ghost

witch

1. Make three standing bats.
2. Make several birds.
3. Make several witches.
4. Make two ghosts.

36

# Thanksgiving Songs

## Turkey Song

*(Sing to the tune of "Oats, Peas, Beans.")*

On Grandpa's farm there's a turkey grand.

He struts around with his tail like a fan.

He gobbles at the girls, he gobbles at the boys.

He thinks he's singing; it sounds like noise.

Thanksgiving Day will soon be here.

When we give thanks for all things dear.

We'll fix our food, bless everyone.

Then we'll do the gobbling.

Thanksgiving Day is fun.

## Gobble, Gobble, Gobble

*(Sing to the tune of "Did You Ever See a Lassie?")*

Gobble, gobble, gobble, fat turkeys, fat turkeys.

Gobble, gobble, gobble, fat turkeys are we.

As sure as we're living, we're here for Thanksgiving.

Gobble, gobble, gobble, fat turkeys are we.

## I Like Celery

*(To the tune of "Skip to My Lou.")*

I like celery, how about you?

I like celery, how about you?

I like celery, how about you?

I like celery, boop-boop-dee-doo!

**Teacher Suggestions:** Show examples of real foods during "I Like Celery." Later, the children may be given the foods to sample during snack time. Sing the song many times using other fall foods, for example, squash, cranberries, turkey, etc.

Use the patterns on page 38 to create a paper bag turkey for "Turkey Song" and "Gobble, Gobble, Gobble."

# Patterns for Thanksgiving Songs

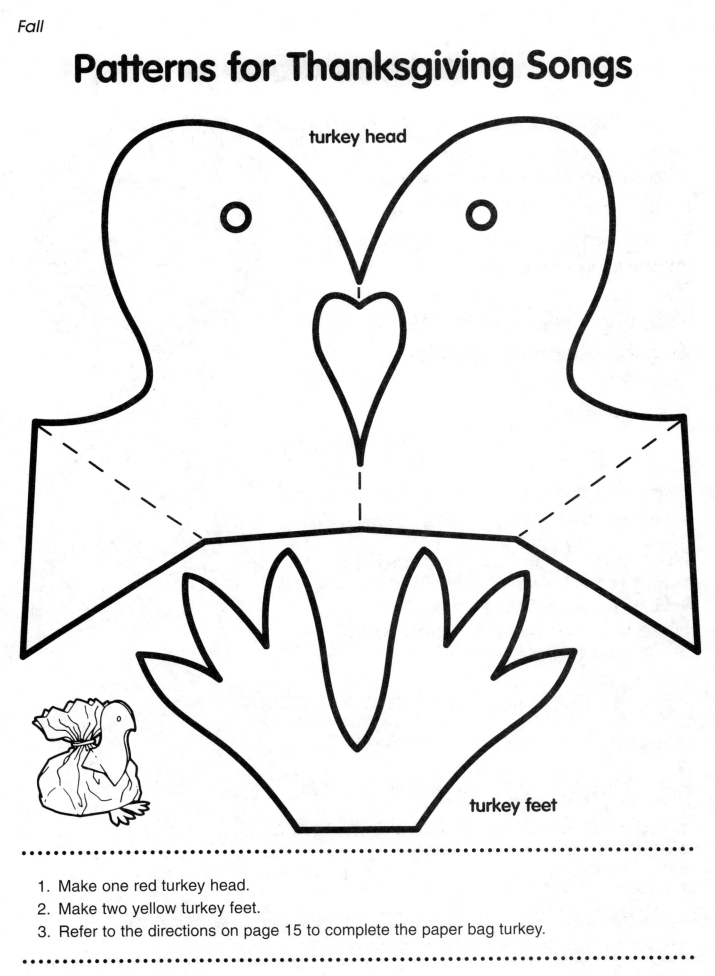

turkey head

turkey feet

1. Make one red turkey head.
2. Make two yellow turkey feet.
3. Refer to the directions on page 15 to complete the paper bag turkey.

# Turkey Poems

## A Turkey

**The turkey is a funny bird.**
*(Place the turkey on the flannelboard.)*

**His head goes wobble, wobble.**
*(Wobble the turkey's head.)*

**The only thing that he can say . . .**

**Is gobble, gobble, gobble!**
*(Have the children join in and make the gobble noise.)*

## The Turkey

**Here is a turkey, just see his tail spread.**
*(Hold your hands and fingers up with fingers open.)*

**Here is an apple, so juicy and red.**
*(Make a circle with your fingers and thumb.)*

**Here is a pumpkin, big and round.**
*(Make a big circle using your arms.)*

**Here are the leaves that drift to the ground.**
*(Place your hands above your head. Move your hands back and forth above your head and then down to the floor.)*

**For all these things, so bright and gay,**

**We give our thanks on Thanksgiving Day.**
*(Fold your hands as if you were praying.)*

Use the patterns on pages 18 and 40 to create the turkey, apple, pumpkin, and leaf flannel pieces. Use the patterns in conjunction with the hand motions.

# Patterns for Turkey Poems

turkey

apple

pumpkin

1. Make one turkey.
2. Make several different fall-colored leaves using the patterns on page 18.
3. Make one apple.
4. Make one pumpkin.

# White Feather, White Feather

*(Patterned after the rhyme "Brown Bear, Brown Bear" by Bill Martin.)*

**White feather, white feather, what do you see?**

*(Place the turkey's body on the flannelboard.  Place the white feather on the far left side of the turkey's back.)*

**I see a gold feather next to me.**

*(Place the gold feather right next to the white feather.)*

**Gold feather, gold feather, what do you see?**

**I see a blue feather next to me.**

*(Place the blue feather right next to the gold feather.)*

**Blue feather, blue feather, what do you see?**

**I see a red feather next to me.**

*(Place the red feather right next to the blue feather.)*

**Red feather, red feather, what do you see?**

**I see a brown feather next to me.**

*(Place the brown feather right next to the red feather.)*

**Brown feather, brown feather, what do you see?**

**I see an orange feather next to me.**

*(Place the orange feather right next to the brown feather.)*

**Orange feather, orange feather, what do you see?**

**I see a yellow feather next to me.**

*(Place the yellow feather right next to the orange feather.)*

**Yellow feather, yellow feather, what do you see?**

**I see a green feather next to me.**

*(Place the green feather right next to the yellow feather.)*

**Green feather, green feather, what do you see?**

**I see a black feather next to me.**

*(Place the black feather right next to the green feather.)*

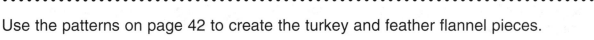

Use the patterns on page 42 to create the turkey and feather flannel pieces.

# Patterns for White Feather, White Feather

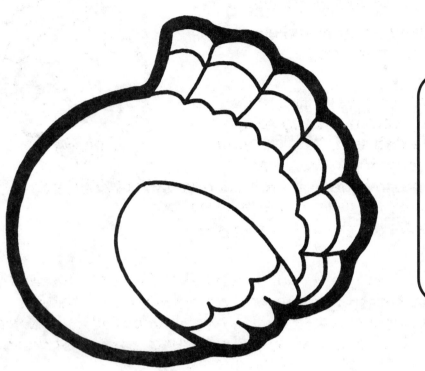

**turkey body**

**turkey feet**

**turkey head**

**turkey feather**

1. Make one brown turkey body and one brown turkey head with a red wattle.
2. Make two gold feet.
3. Glue the head and feet onto the turkey's body.
4. Make one feather in each of the following colors:  white, gold, blue, red, brown, orange, yellow, green, and black.

# Tommy Turkey

**Tommy was a beautiful, big, fat turkey who lived on a farm.**
*(Place the barn and the brown turkey on the flannelboard.)*

**One day just before Thanksgiving, Tommy Turkey went for a walk. On the way he met a dog.**
*(Place the dog on the flannelboard.)*

**The dog said, "Ha Ha! Ho Ho! Hee Hee! You're the funniest turkey I ever did see." Tommy Turkey said, "What's wrong with me?" The dog said, "Look at your ugly color. You'd be much prettier if you were red."
So Tommy Turkey hurried home and dyed his feathers a beautiful bright red.**
*(Remove the brown turkey and put the red turkey on the flannelboard.)*

**Red Tommy Turkey walked down the street and met a cat.**
*(Put the cat on the flannelboard.)*

**The cat looked at him and said, "Ha Ha! Ho Ho! Hee Hee! You're the funniest turkey I ever did see." Tommy Turkey said, "What's wrong with me?" The cat said, "Whoever heard of a red turkey? You'd be much more beautiful if you were green." So Tommy Turkey hurried home and dyed his feathers a beautiful green.**
*(Remove the red turkey and put the green turkey on the flannelboard.)*

**While he was out walking, he met a cow who said, "Ha Ha! Ho Ho! Hee Hee! You're the funniest turkey I ever did see." Green Tommy Turkey said, "I am? What's wrong with me now?" "Whoever heard of a green turkey?" said the cow, "You'd be much more attractive if you were orange." So Tommy Turkey hurried home and dyed his feathers a beautiful orange.**
*(Remove the green turkey and put the orange turkey on the flannelboard.)*

**Orange Tommy Turkey said, "Now I am the most beautiful turkey in the world." But soon he met a sheep and a horse who looked at him and said, "Ha Ha! Ho Ho! Hee Hee! You're the funniest turkey we ever did see."**
*(Put the sheep and the horse on the flannelboard.)*

**Tommy Turkey, with tears in his eyes, said, "What's the matter with me?" The sheep and the horse answered, "Look at your color. You'd be much more beautiful if you were brown. Come back to the barn with us and we will turn you into the most beautiful turkey in the world." Tommy Turkey went with them, and before you could say "Old Mac Donald" he had turned into the most beautiful brown turkey you have ever seen.**
*(Remove the orange turkey and put the brown turkey back on the flannelboard.)*

• • • • • • • • • • • • • • • • • • • • • • • • • • • • • • • • • • • • • • • • • • • • • • • • • •

Use the patterns on pages 40, 44, and 45 to create the patterns needed.

• • • • • • • • • • • • • • • • • • • • • • • • • • • • • • • • • • • • • • • • • • • • • • • • • •

# Patterns for Tommy Turkey

dog

barn

cat

1. Make one barn. Enlarge the barn if possible.

2. Make one dog.

3. Make one cat.

4. Make one turkey in each of the following colors: brown, red, green, and orange, using the pattern on page 40.

# Patterns for Tommy Turkey *(cont.)*

cow

sheep

horse

1. Make one cow.
2. Make one sheep.
3. Make one horse.

# Winter Unit

Activities for winter vary depending on the part of the country in which you live. This is an excellent time to enhance vocabulary by discussing the changes in the weather, from rain to sleet to snow. In many of the southern states one would not expect children to know what snow is unless an artificial snow experience was available.

## Teaching Tips

Write the words to finger plays on the back of stick puppets. This allows the teacher to have the words right in front of him or her, instead of memorizing the poem.

Wear an apron with pockets to hold the cards with words to new songs and finger plays and to store finger puppets to use as filler activities when there are a few minutes between activities.

A felt apron can be used when a flannelboard is not available. This is an excellent teaching strategy, especially if you are outside.

## Art Activity

Make an ice sculpture. Fill large containers with water and freeze them. Place the frozen blocks of ice outside in the water table. Ask the children to sprinkle handfuls of rock salt onto the ice blocks. Have them watch carefully as cavities form in the ice. Mix colored water using water and food coloring. Give the children a plastic eyedropper and allow them to drop colored water into the cavities.

Paint with ice. Make a large bowl with ice cubes available. Give each child a pair of tongs. Have 1" squares (2.54 cm) of different-colored tissue paper on a plate. Have the child lift an ice cube out of the bowl using tongs, then place the ice cube on the plate and move it around. The colors will bleed and a beautiful color combination will emerge.

## Supporting Children with Special Needs

Children with special needs require lots of repetition. The winter unit includes several flannelboard stories using the number five (valentines, leprechauns, etc.) Take time to count to five prior to and after each story. When possible, have five children come to the front and hand each an object (a heart for "Five Little Hearts"), then count them. This helps children learn their numbers and it reinforces the concept of one-to-one correspondence.

## Enrichment

Did you know that you can recreate the sound of rain inside? Have children sit in a circle. Tell the children that when you are in front of them, they need to do what you do. Begin walking around the inside of the circle and rubbing your hands together. Walk around the entire circle. When you have reached the place where you began, start snapping your fingers. Walk around the entire circle. When you reach the place where you started, slap your hands on your thighs. Continue around the circle. The gentle rubbing will sound like light rain. As you come to the spot in the circle where you began, start stomping your feet. The stomping will mimic the sound of thunder. You can reverse the movements to signal that the storm is clearing.

## Book Suggestions

Eagle, Kin. *It's Raining, It's Pouring.* Charlesbridge Publishing, Inc., 1997.
Keats, Ezra Jack. *The Snowy Day.* Viking Children's Books, 1996.

# Meeting the Standards: Winter Unit

## Language Arts

- Comprehends what others are saying
- Asks and answers questions
- Demonstrates competency in speaking as a tool for learning
- Demonstrates competency in listening as a tool for learning
- Is developing fine motor skills
- Identifies and sorts common color words into basic categories
- Produces meaningful linguistic sounds
- Produces rhyming words in response to an oral prompt
- Recites familiar stories and rhymes with patterns
- Recognizes colors
- Recognizes color words
- Recognizes meaningful words
- Responds to oral directions
- Responds to oral questions
- Understands that printed material provides information
- Uses picture clues to aid comprehension

## Mathematics

- Conceptualizes one-to-one correspondence
- Divides objects into categories
- Classifies objects
- Connects math with the real world
- Connects math with other disciplines
- Copies and extends patterns
- Describes basic shapes
- Estimates quantities
- Explores activities involving chance
- Identifies equal/unequal portions
- Identifies shapes in the real world
- Implements a problem-solving strategy
- Makes predictions
- Names basic shapes
- Solves simple equations
- Solves basic shapes
- Uses verbal communication
- Uses pictorial communication

## Science

- Applies problem-solving skills
- Discusses changes in seasons
- Identifies objects by color
- Identifies objects by properties
- Identifies objects by shape
- Identifies objects by size
- Identifies color in the real world
- Observes, identifies, and measures objects
- Predicts
- Problem solves through group activities
- Recognizes opposites (wet/dry)

# Five Little Snowmen

## Five little snowmen standing around my door.

*(Put five snowmen and a yellow sun on the flannelboard.)*

## This one melted and then there were four.

*(Point to the snowman as you take it off the flannelboard.)*

## Four little snowmen near a green pine tree.

*(Place the pine tree on the flannelboard.)*

## This one melted and then there were three.

*(Point to the snowman that melted as you take it off the flannelboard.)*

## Three little snowmen with caps and mittens blue.

## This one melted and then there were two.

*(Point to the snowman as you take it off the flannelboard.)*

## Two little snowmen standing in the sun.

## This one melted and then there was one.

*(Point to the snowman as you take it off the flannelboard.)*

## One little snowman started to run,
## But he melted away and then there were none.

*(Take the remaining snowman off the flannelboard.)*

## Why did the snowmen melt?

Use the pattern on page 49 to create the snowmen and pine tree flannel pieces.

# Patterns for Five Little Snowmen

cap

snowman

pine tree

mittens

• • • • • • • • • • • • • • • • • • • • • • • • • • • • • • • • • • • • • • • • • • • • • • •

1. Make one green pine tree.
2. Make five snowmen.  Make caps and blue mittens for each.
3. Make one house with a door using the patterns on page 25.
4. Cut out a yellow circle for the sun.

• • • • • • • • • • • • • • • • • • • • • • • • • • • • • • • • • • • • • • • • • • • • • • •

# Hanukkah Poem

*(Sing to the tune of "One Little, Two Little, Three Little Indians.")*

*(Place the menorah on the flannelboard.)*
**One little, two little, three little candles,**
*(Add the first, second, and third candles to the menorah.)*
**Four little, five little, six little candles,**
*(Add the fourth, fifth, and sixth candles to the menorah.)*
**Seven little, eight little, nine little candles,**
*(Add the seventh, eighth, and ninth candles to the menorah.)*
**In my Hanukkah menorah.**

**The first night, one little candle,**
*(Add a flame to the first candle.)*
**The second night, two little candles,**
*(Add a flame to the second candle.)*
**The third night, three little candles,**
**In my Hanukkah menorah.**
*(Add a flame to the third candle.)*

**The fourth night, four little candles,**
*(Add a flame to the fourth candle.)*
**The fifth night, five little candles,**
*(Add a flame to the fifth candle.)*
**The sixth night, six little candles,**
**In my Hanukkah menorah.**
*(Add a flame to the sixth candle.)*

**The seventh night, seven little candles,**
*(Add a flame to the seventh candle.)*
**The eighth night, eight little candles,**
*(Add a flame to the eighth candle.)*
**And the shammash makes nine little candles,**
**In my Hanukkah menorah.**
*(Add the large center candle, the shammash.)*

• • • • • • • • • • • • • • • • • • • • • • • • • • • • • • • • • • • • • • • •

Use the patterns on page 51 to present the flannelboard story.

**Note:** Explain that the shammash is a very special candle on the menorah. It is used to light the other candles each night. The eight candles symbolize the eight special days celebrated during Hanukkah.

• • • • • • • • • • • • • • • • • • • • • • • • • • • • • • • • • • • • • • • •

# Patterns for Hanukkah Poem

shammash

menorah

1. Make one menorah and decorate it. Try using metallic paper and jewels. Velcro® can be attached to the back to help it stick to the flannelboard.

2. Make one shammash candle.

3. Make eight menorah candles.

4. Make nine flames.

# Christmas Poem

**Up on the chimney Santa Claus crept,**
*(Cup left hand and put first finger of right hand into the left hand.)*

**Into the room where children slept.**
*(Place three fingers of right hand on the palm of your left hand.)*

**He saw their stockings hung in a line,**
*(Three fingers suspended downward from your left hand.)*

**And he filled them with candies and goodies fine.**
*(Make a motion as though filling the stockings.)*

**Although he counted them, one, two, three,**
*(Indicate by counting your fingers.)*

**The baby's stocking he could not see.**
*(Pretend to look around.)*

**"Ho, Ho," said Santa. "That won't do."**
*(Wag your finger back and forth.)*

**So he popped her present right into her shoe.**
*(Cup left hand and put the first finger of the right hand into the left hand.)*

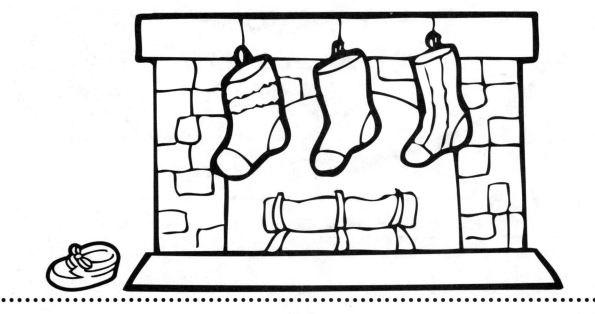

Use the patterns on page 53 to create flannel pieces to supplement the finger movements.

# Patterns for Christmas Poem

shoe

stocking

candy

present

• • • • • • • • • • • • • • • • • • • • • • • • • • • • • • • • • • • • • • •

1. Make three stockings.  Decorate each one using sequins, lace, glitter glue, etc.
2. Make one shoe pattern.
3. Make presents for each stocking and the shoe.  Decorate each one using different colored felt, ribbon, and bows.
4. Make candies for each stocking and shoe.

• • • • • • • • • • • • • • • • • • • • • • • • • • • • • • • • • • • • • • •

# Big Red Heart

*(Sing to the tune of "For He's a Jolly Good Fellow.")*

I have a big red heart.
I have a big red heart.
I have a big red heart.
That I will give to you.
It brings you hugs and kisses.
It brings you hugs and kisses.
It brings you hugs and kisses.
That's because you are my friend.

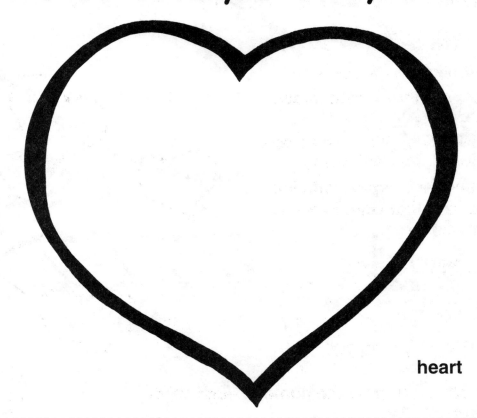

**heart**

**Teacher Suggestion:** Show the children a big red heart. (Enlarge the pattern above.) Give it to one of the children. Sing the song, and continue to repeat it until the heart has been passed to each child.

# Valentine Rhymes

## A Happy Little Heart

**I'm a happy little heart that's pink, white, and red.**
*(Place the pink, white, and red heart on the flannelboard.)*

**A happy little heart with lace around my edge,**
*(Point to the lace around the edge.)*

**I have three words on the front of me
That say, "I love you." Oh, can't you see.**
*(Point to the words "I Love You" printed on the heart.)*

**I'm a happy little heart that's pink,
white, and red.**
*(Place the pink, white, and red heart
on the flannelboard.)*

**A happy little heart with lace around my edge.**
*(Point to the lace around the edge.)*

**I have three words on the front of me.**
*(Point to the words as the children read, "I love you.")*

## Five Little Valentines

*(Sing to the tune of "Five Little Ducks.")*

**Five little valentines that I once knew.**
*(Put five hearts on the flannelboard.)*

**Red ones, white ones, purple ones, too.**
*(Point to the colors as they are stated.)*

**But the valentine that rhymes with ink
Is my favorite, and that color is pink!**
*(Point to the pink heart.)*

## Little Hearts

**This little heart is here to say**
*(Point to one of the hearts.)*

**This little heart loves you today.**
*(Point to the heart that says, "I love you.")*

**These little hearts wish (state the name of each child)
A Happy Valentine's Day.**

• • • • • • • • • • • • • • • • • • • • • • • • • • • • • • • • • • • • • • • • • • • • •

Use the patterns on page 56 to create the heart flannel pieces for each poem.

• • • • • • • • • • • • • • • • • • • • • • • • • • • • • • • • • • • • • • • • • • • • •

# Patterns for Valentine Rhymes

heart

lace background

1. For "A Happy Little Heart," make a pink, white, and red heart with lace around the edge. Use glitter glue pens to write the words, "I love you" on the heart.

2. For "Five Little Valentines," make one heart in each of the following colors: red, white, lavender, purple, and pink.

3. For "Little Hearts," make three hearts, each in a different color. Use a felt pen to write the words "I love you" on one of the hearts.

# Valentine Games

## My Valentine

I have bought a valentine,

Pink and lacy and blue.

It is the one I like the best,

And so I'll give it to you.

**Teacher Suggestion:** Practice the verse while children are sitting in a circle. While the class repeats the verse, have a child come up to walk around the inside of the circle holding the valentine. The child gives the valentine to a classmate and sits back down. Repeat.

Quiet as a little mouse,

I am going to the house

The house of a very special friend

To leave a valentine.

**Teacher Suggestion:** Have the children sit in a circle. Instruct them to place their hands palms up, on their laps. One child is given a valentine with a mouse attached. He or she tiptoes around the outside of the circle and leaves it behind a friend. The first child sits where the friend was and the friend takes his or her turn.

• • • • • • • • • • • • • • • • • • • • • • • • • • • • • • • • • • • • • • • • • • • • • •

Use the patterns on page 58 to create the valentine and mouse tagboard pieces.

• • • • • • • • • • • • • • • • • • • • • • • • • • • • • • • • • • • • • • • • • • • • • •

# Patterns for Valentine Games

mouse

valentine

. . . . . . . . . . . . . . . . . . . . . . . . . . . . . . . . . . . . . . . . . . . . . . . .

1. For "My Valentine," use the patterns above to make a pink lacy heart out of heavy tagboard.  Add blue ribbon decorations to the heart.

2. For "Quiet as a Little Mouse" use heavy tagboard to create one valentine.  Make one mouse.  Attach the mouse to the valentine.

. . . . . . . . . . . . . . . . . . . . . . . . . . . . . . . . . . . . . . . . . . . . . . . .

# The Tasty, Pasty Valentine

**Little Gray Mouse looked around his cozy little house.**
*(Put Gray Mouse on the flannelboard.)*

**Oh, I am the lucky one, he thought. He was lucky. His little hole in the wall was just right. The house he lived in was just right, too. People lived in the house—a mother and a father, a boy and a girl.**
*(Put the boy and the girl on the flannelboard.)*

**But Gray Mouse did not mind that. "They are nice, quiet people." Gray Mouse told his friends, "They don't give me much trouble." And they did have a fine kitchen. A fellow could always pick up a little snack at bedtime. Little Gray Mouse lived in a hole in the wall of the boy's room. That was lucky, too. For the boy left some good crumbs! Bread crumbs with peanut butter! Yum!**

**But sometimes the boy would stay in his room—right in Gray Mouse's way. That was the trouble right now. Mouse wanted to go down to the kitchen. He wanted to go very much, for he could smell the cheese!**
*(Place the cheese on the flannelboard.)*

**Lovely, lovely cheese! But the boy was in the room. So was the girl. They were standing at the table, working. Why don't they go out to play? Little Gray Mouse thought crossly. But the boy and girl went on working. They had red paper and white paste and scissors. Snip! Snip! They cut up the red paper. Swoosh! Swoosh! Swoosh! They put paste on the red paper, here and there.**
*(Put several valentines on the flannelboard.)*

**The children talked about making valentines for their friends. The little boy said, "Let's finish up, then we can go out and play." Yes, indeed! thought Little Gray Mouse. Do go away!**
*(Ask the children why the mouse wanted the children to go away.)*

**Teacher Suggestion:** Follow up the activity by having the children make valentines to give their classmates. Use the patterns on page 60 to create the girl, boy, table, and cheese flannel pieces. Use the mouse pattern on page 68.

# Patterns for The Tasty, Pasty Valentine

girl

boy

table

cheese wedge

1. Make one girl and one boy.
2. Make one table.
3. Make one cheese wedge.
4. Make one mouse using the pattern on page 58.
5. Make several valentines using the patterns on page 58.

# Pitter Patter Rain Story

One day it rained.  Pitter patter, it rained on the town.  Pitter patter, it rained on the ground.

Pitter patter, pitter patter, it rained on a truck that went rumbling through town.
*(Place the truck on the flannelboard.)*

Rumble rumble, it rained and it rained and the truck got all wet.  Pitter patter, pitter patter, it rained on an airplane that was brumming through the sky.
*(Put the airplane on the flannelboard.)*

Brum, brum, it rained and it rained, and the airplane got all wet.  Pitter patter, pitter patter, it rained on a cow that was mooing in the pasture.
*(Put the cow on the flannelboard.)*

Moo, moo, it rained and it rained and the cow got all wet.  Pitter patter, pitter patter, it rained on a duck that was quacking on the lake.
*(Place the duck on the flannelboard.)*

Quack, quack, it rained and it rained and the duck got all wet.  Pitter patter, pitter patter, it rained on a sailboat that was flip flopping its sails on the lake.
*(Place the sailboat on the flannelboard.)*

Flip, flop, it rained and it rained and the sailboat got all wet.  Pitter patter, pitter patter, it rained on a train that was puff chuffing down the track.
*(Put the train on the flannelboard.)*

Puff, chuff, it rained and it rained and the train got all wet.  Then down the road came a boy and girl.
*(Place the boy and the girl in rain gear on the flannelboard.)*

They wore rain coats, rain hats, and high boots and carried umbrellas.  Splash, splash, they walked through the puddles.  The boy's raincoat got all wet.  The rain hat got all wet and the high boots got all wet.  The boy's umbrella got all wet.  Did the boy get all wet?  No, he stayed dry.

Splash, splash, they walked through the puddles.  The girl's raincoat got all wet.  The rain hat got all wet and the high boots got all wet.  The girl's umbrella got all wet.  Did the girl get all wet?  No, she stayed dry.

Use the patterns on pages 62–64 to create Pitter Patter Rain Story flannel pieces.

# Patterns for
# Pitter Patter Rain Story

airplane

duck

truck

· · · · · · · · · · · · · · · · · · · · · · · · · · · · · · · · · · · · · · · · · · ·

1. Make one truck.
2. Make one airplane.
3. Make one cow using the pattern on page 45.
4. Make one duck.

· · · · · · · · · · · · · · · · · · · · · · · · · · · · · · · · · · · · · · · · · · ·

# Patterns for
# Pitter Patter Rain Story *(cont.)*

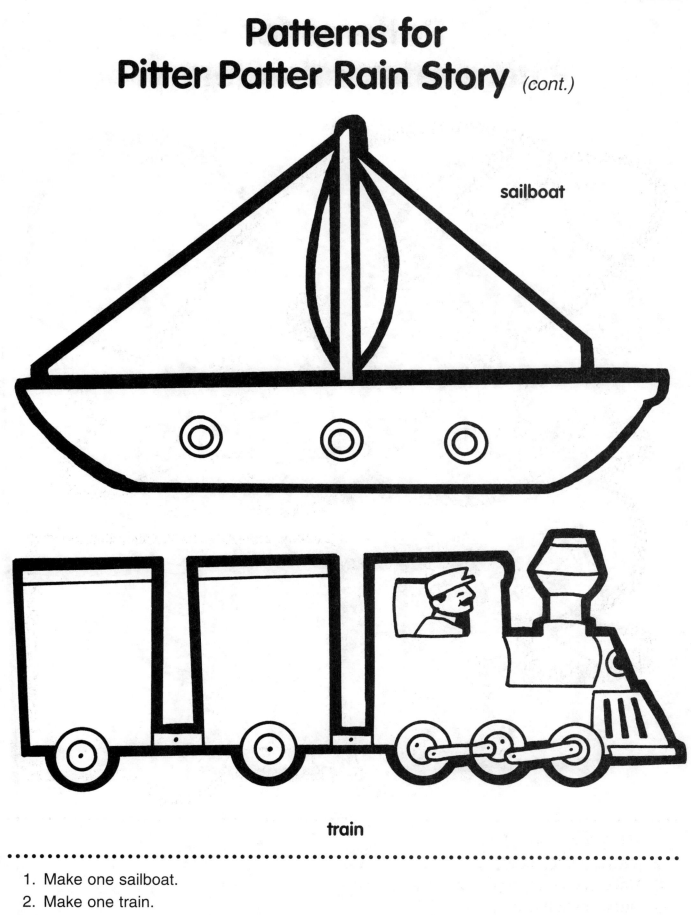

sailboat

train

..............................................................

1. Make one sailboat.
2. Make one train.

..............................................................

# Patterns for
# Pitter Patter Rain Story *(cont.)*

**girl**                    **boy**

1. Make one boy wearing rain gear.
2. Make one girl wearing rain gear.

# Rain Elf

Rain, rain, rain, rain,
Pouring on our roof!
Sounds like racing horses,
Thundering on the hoof!

Roar, roar, rumble, roar,
The clatter it does make!
I really fear the thunderclouds
Are playing pat-a-cake.

Rain, rain, rain, rain,
Down my windowpane!
Run, run, run, run,
Down the water drain.

Do you suppose that someone…
A water elf no doubt!
Has pulled the stopper in the clouds.
And let the water out?

..................................................................................................

**Teacher Suggestion:** Discuss with the children what they think the elf in the poem looks like. Have the children think about what the elf is doing in the clouds and if someone really could pull a stopper out in the clouds to release the rain. Then have the children illustrate this fun poem.

..................................................................................................

# Five Little Leprechauns

*(Place the tree and the grass on the flannelboard.)*

**Five little leprechauns scurrying by my door,**
*(Place the five leprechauns on the flannelboard.)*

**One jumped away, and then there were four.**
*(Remove one leprechaun.)*

**Four tiny leprechauns, climbing in my tree,**
*(Place four leprechauns on a tree.)*

**One hid in green grass, and then
there were three.**
*(Move one leprechaun behind the grass.)*

**Three wee leprechauns, just a busy few,**
*(Move three leprechauns to the grass area.)*

**One went to find the pot of gold, and then there were two.**
*(Remove one leprechaun.)*

**Two frisky leprechauns having lots of fun,**
*(Dance two leprechauns around.)*

**One roamed away, and then there was one.**
*(Remove one leprechaun.)*

**One funny leprechaun with
all his work done,**

**Slipped off for a nap and
then there were none!**
*(Remove the last leprechaun.)*

Use the patterns on page 67 to create the leprechaun flannel pieces.

# Patterns for
# Five Little Leprechauns

five leprechauns

1. Make five little leprechauns.
2. Make one tree using the pattern on page 20.
3. Make a patch of grass using the pattern on page 86.

# Spring Unit

Spring and science experiences go hand in hand. Children love to plant seeds, water the garden, and watch plants grow. The opportunity to observe the metamorphosis of a butterfly from caterpillar to chrysalis to butterfly (or moth from caterpillar to cocoon to moth) is a wonderful opportunity. Encourage children to discuss how butterflies and moths are alike and how they are different. Compare chrysalises and cocoons. Note that butterflies rest with their wings up, and moths rest with their wings down flat. Encourage advanced language as discussions of nature unfold.

## Teaching Tip

For teachers in traditional programs, spring is a season representing the end of the school year. Now that the children have seen many puppets, allow them to create their own versions. Have the children cut out two small bunnies, eggs, or birds. Give each child one craft stick and one Styrofoam cup with a hole cut in the bottom. (The stick will go through the hole.) Have each child decorate his or her characters and glue them to the stick—one on each side. Use the puppets to act out the spring poems included in this unit.

## Art Activity

Egg painting is a wonderful activity for springtime. Cut out large egg shapes and paint them with pastel paints. Use different sized eggs. Cotton swabs can be used for smaller shapes and finger paints work well for larger eggs. You might even try blow-painting eggs. Use straws to blow drops of watered-down paint around the egg-shaped paper.

## Supporting Children with Special Needs

Sometimes children with special needs get lost in the activities of the season and need specific activities to integrate previously learned concepts. Try playing a simple counting game with plastic eggs. Put small objects in the plastic eggs and place the eggs in a basket. Allow each child to choose one egg, open it, and tell you what is inside. Count how many objects there are inside. Party supply and cake decorating stores sell many small inexpensive objects. This activity is a wonderful, enjoyable language development task and it reinforces counting for mathematics.

## Enrichment

Give each child a piece of cardboard and materials such as sticks, straw, raffia, packaging materials, yarn, string, etc. Let each child make his or her own bird's nest. Talk about how the birds use their beaks to make their nests. Go on a walk and determine other objects that can be used to create a nest.

## Book Suggestions

Grosset, Yvonne Hooker. *The Little Green Caterpillar*. Grosset & Dunlap Publishers, 1989.

Heller, Ruth. *Chickens Aren't the Only Ones*. Turtleback Books, 1999.

# Meeting the Standards: Spring Unit

## Language Arts

- Listens
- Comprehends what others are saying
- Asks and answers questions
- Demonstrates competency in speaking
- Demonstrates competency in listening
- Follows simple directions
- Identifies and sorts common words into basic categories
- Identifies characters, settings, and important events
- Produces meaningful linguistic sounds
- Produces rhyming words in response to an oral prompt
- Recites familiar stories and rhymes with patterns
- Recites short stories
- Recognizes colors
- Recognizes color words
- Recognizes meaningful words
- Responds to oral directions
- Responds to oral questions
- Retells familiar stories
- Auditorily tracks each word in a sentence
- Understands that printed material provides information
- Uses picture clues to aid comprehension
- Uses picture clues to make predictions about content

## Mathematics

- Conceptualizes one-to-one correspondence
- Compares whole numbers
- Connects math with the real world
- Connects math with other disciplines
- Copies and extends patterns
- Counts to ten
- Describes basic shapes
- Estimates quantities
- Explores activities involving chance
- Identifies equal/unequal portions
- Identifies shapes in the real world
- Identifies shapes in different positions
- Implements a problem-solving strategy
- Is learning number names
- Makes predictions
- Names basic shapes
- Recognizes and collects data
- Solves simple equations
- Sorts basic shapes
- Uses verbal communication
- Uses pictorial communication
- Uses symbolic communication
- Understands the problem

## Science

- Applies problem-solving skills
- Classifies
- Communicates
- Discusses changes in seasons
- Identifies objects by color
- Identifies objects by properties

- Identifies objects by shape
- Identifies objects by size
- Identifies color in the real world
- Observes and identifies objects
- Predicts
- Problem solves through group activities

# My Garden

## Here is my garden; I'll rake it with care.

*(Show a raking motion using both of your arms.)*

## And then some flower seeds, I'll plant there.

*(Pretend to plant the seeds in the soil.)*

## The sun will shine, and the rain will fall.

*(Form a circle with both of your hands and hold them overhead to suggest the sun, then bring your hands down, wiggling fingers to simulate the rain.)*

## My garden will blossom and grow straight and tall.

*(Pretend to be a plant, sprouting and growing.)*

# Little Brown Seeds

## Little brown seeds so small and round,

*(Pretend to hold a seed in your hand.)*

## Are sleeping quietly under the ground.

*(Place palms together beside your face.)*

## Down come the raindrops, sprinkle, sprinkle, sprinkle.

*(Raise and lower your arms slowly, moving fingers rapidly.)*

## Out comes the rainbow, twinkle, twinkle, twinkle.

*(Draw a big arc in the air.)*

## Little brown seeds way down below,

*(Scrunch down and touch the ground.)*

## Up through the earth they grow, grow, grow.

*(Have the children bend to the floor and rise slowly.)*

## Little green leaves come one by one.

*(Have children extend their arms halfway, one at a time.)*

## They hold up their heads and look at the sun.

*(Have the children look up and extend their arms as far as they can.)*

# The Little Seed

Far down in Mother Earth a tiny little seed lay asleep in a nice warm jacket.

(*Place the sleeping seed on the flannelboard.*)

The seed had been asleep for a long, long time. Now, somebody thought it should wake up. This somebody was an earthworm who lived close by.

(*Place the worm on the flannelboard.*)

He had been creeping about and had seen that all the other little seeds in the neighborhood had roused themselves and were pushing their roots down into the earth and lifting their heads up through the soil into the nice bright sunshine and fresh air of springtime. So when the worm saw this sleepyhead seed, he cried, "Wake up! Every one of your neighbors is awake and growing."

"How can I grow in this tight jacket?" said the sleepy little seed. "Push it off," said the worm. The little seed tried and tried, but the jacket wouldn't break.

(*Take the sleeping seed off, and replace it with the struggling seed.*)

All this time the worm was telling him how happy all the other seeds were now that they had lifted their heads into the sunshine. "Oh dear, oh dear, I will never see the sunshine and smell the fresh air," said the little seed with a yawn and promptly fell back asleep. He slept soundly for a long time, but when he woke he found his jacket soft and wet, and when he moved about, his jacket fell off altogether.

(*Take the struggling seed off the flannelboard, and replace it with the happy seed.*)

He felt so warm and happy he cried out, "Who are my friends that have helped me get ready to grow?"

# The Little Seed *(cont.)*

"I helped you, I helped you," said a little voice.

"I'm a sunbeam.  My friends the raindrops and I came down to help you grow."

*(Place the sun and the raindrops on the flannelboard.)*

"How did you know I was here?" asked the seed.

"We just did," said the sunbeam.

"How can I thank you for helping me grow?" asked the little seed.

"Oh, just grow into the very best plant you can," said the sun and the raindrops.

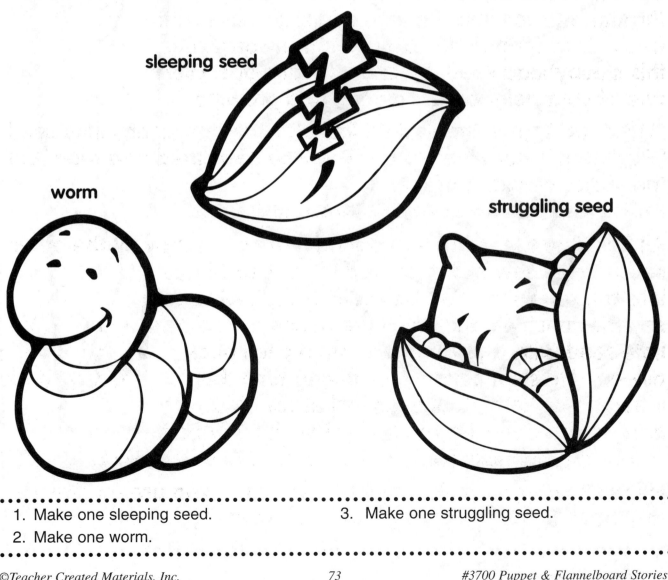

sleeping seed

worm

struggling seed

1. Make one sleeping seed.
2. Make one worm.
3. Make one struggling seed.

# Patterns for The Little Seed

sun ray

raindrops

sun

happy seed

........................................................

1. Make one happy seed with jacket.
2. Make one sun.
3. Make a few raindrops.
4. Make additional rays for the sun.

........................................................

# Caterpillar Story

**This is the story of a little caterpillar.  He was very hungry so he crawled out on a leaf, and he ate, and he ate, and he ate.**

*(Move your sock caterpillar puppet as if it is eating.  Pretend to "eat" the children.  Only touch those children who are comfortable with touching.)*

**He ate so much that soon his skin began to feel tight, so he shook, and he shook, and he shook and do you know what happened?**

*(Shake your whole body.  Encourage the children to shake with you.)*

**His skin fell off.  He looked down and do you know what?  He had a brand new skin.**

**He felt hungry again, so he crawled over to a new leaf, and he ate, and he ate, and he ate, and he ate.**

*(Move your sock caterpillar puppet as if it is eating.  Pretend to "eat" the children.)*

**He ate so much that soon his new skin began to feel tight, so he shook, and he shook, and he shook, and his skin fell off again.**

*(Shake your whole body.  Encourage the children to shake with you.)*

**He looked down and do you know what?  He had another new skin.**

**He felt hungry again, so he crawled over to a new leaf, and he ate, and ate, and he ate, and he ate.**

*(Move the puppet as if it is eating.  Pretend to "eat" the children.)*

**He ate so much that soon his new skin began to feel tight, so he shook and he shook, and he shook, and his skin fell off again.**

. . . . . . . . . . . . . . . . . . . . . . . . . . . . . . . . . . . . . . . . . . . . . . . . . . . . . . . . . . . . . . . .

Use the flannelboard patterns on page 77 or tell this story using a a caterpillar made out of a sock and a felt butterfly.

**Teacher Suggestion:** Before you present this story, put the butterfly inside the sock puppet. The sock can be made into the chrysalis by pulling the opening of the sock up until it covers the toe (which is the head of your caterpillar).  Pull the butterfly out at the end of the story. Only tell this story once a day though, or it loses its magic for the children.

. . . . . . . . . . . . . . . . . . . . . . . . . . . . . . . . . . . . . . . . . . . . . . . . . . . . . . . . . . . . . . . .

# Caterpillar Story *(cont.)*

**He looked down and do you know what? He had another new skin.**

*(Shake your whole body. Encourage the children to shake with you.)*

**He was hungry again, so he crawled over to a new leaf, and he ate, and he ate, and he ate, and he ate.**

*(Move the puppet as if it is eating. Pretend to "eat" the children.)*

**He ate so much that soon his new skin began to feel tight. By now he wasn't a little caterpillar any more. He was a big caterpillar. This time he did not shake and shake. Instead, he crawled out on the tree limb. He fastened himself to the limb and he began to spin.**

*(The sock puppet will crawl up your arm as you extend your arm upward, bent at the elbow. With your fingers grasped at the end of the sock, move your hand in a circular motion and gradually encase the sock puppet. Be careful not to expose the butterfly under the sock.)*

**He spun, and he spun, and he spun. Soon he was all wrapped up. He had spun a chrysalis and he hung attached to the tree limb. It looked like he was dead.**

**He hung there for a couple of weeks. And then, one day, the chrysalis started to wiggle. It wiggled a little more, and wiggled a little more, and out came the most beautiful butterfly you have ever seen.**

*(Pull the butterfly out of the sock and mimic a flying motion.)*

· · · · · · · · · · · · · · · · · · · · · · · · · · · · · · · · · · · · · · · · · ·

**Teacher Suggestion:** Use the patterns on page 77 to create the butterfly and leaf flannel pieces for a flannelboard version of "Caterpillar Story."

1. Make one caterpillar.
2. Make one chrysalis.
3. Make one butterfly.
4. Make one leaf.

· · · · · · · · · · · · · · · · · · · · · · · · · · · · · · · · · · · · · · · · · ·

# Patterns for Caterpillar Story

butterfly

leaf

chrysalis

caterpillar

# Arabella Miller

Arabella Miller was a fuzzy caterpillar.

First she crawled on my mother,

Then she crawled on my brother.

Little Arabella Miller was a fuzzy caterpillar.

## Directions for a Fuzzy Caterpillar

**Materials:** Nine pompoms with holes, two wooden sticks or dowels, string or yarn, two wiggly eyes or felt circles, glue

**Optional:** beads and decorations

1. String all the pompoms and tie a knot (or attach a bead) at each end.

2. Glue eyes and decorations to the head of the caterpillar.

3. Attach one end of the pompom string to each stick.

**Note to Teacher:** Refer to the cover for a rendering of a fuzzy caterpillar. To manipulate the caterpillar, hold the bottoms of the sticks and move them close together and out again in a gentle manner.

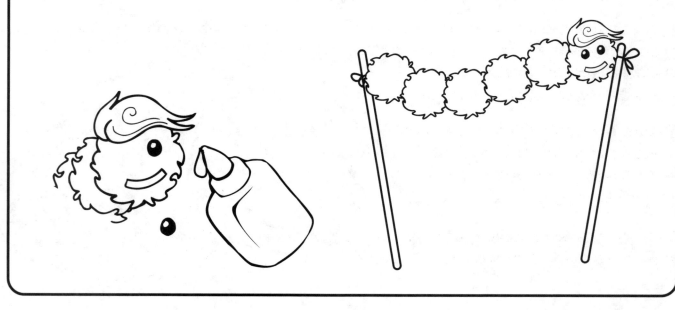

# Lydia Ladybug

*(Begin the story with Lydia Ladybug and Red Rose on the flannelboard.)*

Lydia Ladybug lived in a lovely garden. She was busy and happy all day long. One day she heard Red Rose whispering to her friend, "I wonder why Lydia Ladybug has only one spot?" Sure enough, Lydia looked back and on her pretty red coat was but one black spot. Then she looked at her other ladybug friends. Yes, they had many black spots.

Lydia Ladybug felt so sad that she flew from the garden into the woods, where she stopped to rest on a large toadstool.

*(Place the toadstool on the flannelboard.)*

Then suddenly, she heard a voice from beneath it say, "Lydia Ladybug, I am a magic elf and I know why you are sad. If you would like to feel happy once more, say this magic poem with me.

> 'If these magic words you will heed,
> Each day do just one kind deed.
> You'll be happy and have lots of fun,
> And spots you will have, more than one.'"

After repeating these words, Lydia Ladybug flew off to follow this advice.

*(Place the black ant with the bread crumb on the flannelboard.)*

On the first day, she saw a small black ant who was carrying a bread crumb but had gotten it stuck in a crack. "I'll help you," called Lydia, and she pulled and pulled until the bread crumb came loose and the little ant went on its way.

Lydia Ladybug felt happy, and as she flew on her way over a little pool, she glanced down. To her surprise, she saw that she had not one, but two lovely spots on her red coat.

*(Place the second dot on Lydia Ladybug's back.)*

Before she could think more about it, she heard a voice calling, "Please help me!" She looked about to discover a little green frog.

*(Put the green frog on the flannelboard.)*

The little frog was pulling and tugging to untangle a piece of string that was caught around his foot.

# Lydia Ladybug *(cont.)*

"I will help you," cried Lydia, and she flew down and worked and worked until the little frog was free.  "Thank you, Lydia Ladybug," said the little frog.  Then he said, "Why, Lydia, you have three lovely black spots on your pretty red coat." Sure enough, there were.

*(Place the third dot on Lydia Ladybug's back.)*

As Lydia flew on, she heard a faint little peep.  She stopped to investigate and there in the grass under the big tree was a baby bird that had toppled out of his nest.  *(Place the baby bird on the flannelboard.)*

"Do not cry," said Lydia, "I will find your mother," and she hurriedly flew about until she found Mother and Father Bird.  They were very happy indeed to find their lost baby, and as Lydia flew away, she glanced about at her coat and sure enough, she now had four lovely black spots on her red coat.

*(Place the fourth dot on Lydia Ladybug's back.)*

That night it rained.  The next morning as Lydia crawled from beneath her leaf bed she heard a voice calling, "Oh, my pretty wings are so wet that I can no longer fly."  There was a beautiful butterfly, wings drooping from the rain and dew.

*(Place the butterfly on the flannelboard.)*

"I will help you," called Lydia, and she fanned the butterfly with her little wings until the moving air had dried the pretty butterfly.

Lydia was very tired but as she flew away, she heard Butterfly call, "Thank you, Lydia Ladybug, and what a beautiful coat you are wearing today."

*(Place the fifth dot on Lydia Ladybug's back.)*

And to Lydia Ladybug's delight, there were five lovely spots on her pretty red coat.  Lydia flew off saying,

> "If these magic words you'll heed,
>
> Each day do just one kind deed;
>
> You'll be happy and have lots of fun,
>
> And spots you will have, more than one."

1. Make one Lydia Ladybug.
2. Make five black spots.
3. Make one frog.

4. Make one bird.
5. Make one toadstool.
6. Make one black ant carrying a bread crumb.

# Patterns for Lydia Ladybug

spots

bird

Lydia Ladybug

frog

ant

toadstool

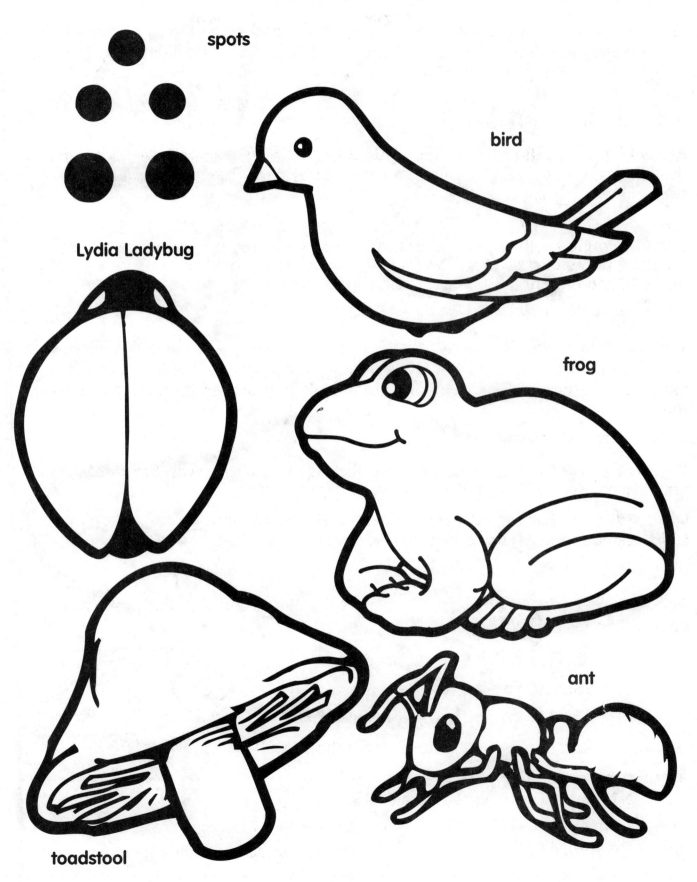

# Patterns for Lydia Ladybug *(cont.)*

**butterfly**

**Red Rose**

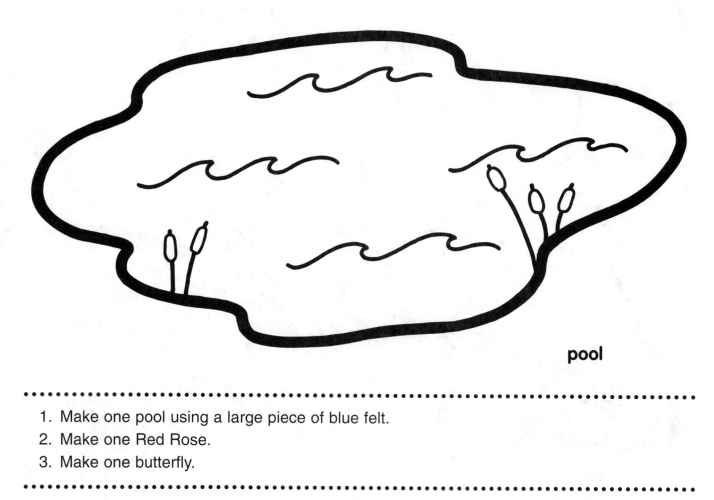

**pool**

1. Make one pool using a large piece of blue felt.
2. Make one Red Rose.
3. Make one butterfly.

# Here's a Bunny

Here's a bunny with ears so funny,

And here's his hole in the ground.

When a noise he hears,

He pricks up his ears

And jumps into his hole in the ground.

bunny

· · · · · · · · · · · · · · · · · · · · · · · · · · · · · · · · · · · · · · · · · · · · · · · · · · · · · · · · · · · · · · · · · · · · ·

**Teacher Suggestion:** To suggest a hole in the ground use a round piece of brown fabric.
The bunny can be placed behind or in front, depending on your storytelling style.

· · · · · · · · · · · · · · · · · · · · · · · · · · · · · · · · · · · · · · · · · · · · · · · · · · · · · · · · · · · · · · · · · · · · ·

# Bunny, Fluffy Bunny

Bunny, fluffy bunny, your eyes are very pink.

Bunny, fluffy bunny, mine are blue, I think.

Bunny, fluffy bunny, your ears are straight and tall.

Bunny, fluffy bunny, mine are short and small.

Bunny, fluffy bunny, you hop to have your fun.

Bunny, fluffy bunny, I just walk and run.

Bunny, fluffy bunny, you eat carrots, lettuce, too.

Bunny, fluffy bunny, in that way I am like you.

Use the patterns on page 85 to create stick puppets.

# Patterns for Bunny, Fluffy Bunny

bunny

carrot

lettuce

........................................................................

1. Make one bunny with a pink eye.
2. Make several carrots.
3. Make one head of lettuce.

........................................................................

# Hopping in the Grass

Who's that hopping in the tall grass?

Hop, hop, hopping in the grass.

It's the bunny rabbit hopping,

Hop, hop, hopping in the grass.

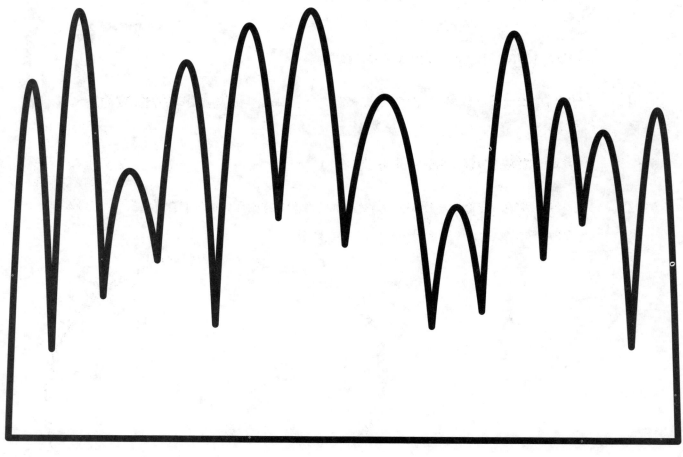

**grass**

Use the bunny pattern on page 85 and the pattern above to create the bunny and grass pieces.

# Five Little Eggs

**Five little eggs, lovely colors wore.**

*(Place five little eggs on the flannelboard.)*

**Mother ate the blue one, and then there were four.**

*(Take the blue egg off the flannelboard.)*

**Four little eggs, two and two you see,**

**Daddy ate the red one, and then there were three.**

*(Take the red egg off the flannelboard.)*

**Three little eggs, before I knew,**

**Sister ate the yellow one, and then there were two.**

*(Take the yellow egg off the flannelboard.)*

**Two little eggs, oh what fun,**

**Brother ate the purple one, and then there was one.**

*(Take the purple egg off the flannelboard.)*

**One little egg, see me run,**

**I ate the green one, and then there were none.**

*(Take the green egg off the flannelboard).*

**egg**

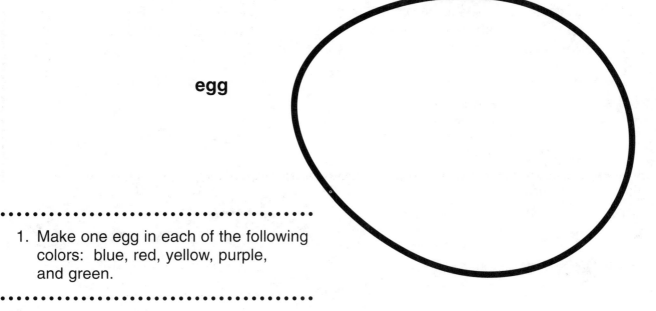

. . . . . . . . . . . . . . . . . . . . . . . . . . . . . . . . .

1. Make one egg in each of the following
colors:  blue, red, yellow, purple,
and green.

. . . . . . . . . . . . . . . . . . . . . . . . . . . . . . . . .

# Summer Unit

Summer is the time for water play and lots of outdoor activities. Discuss camping, vacations, and travel with the children. When it is too hot outside, set up a campground with a tent and camping props indoors. Or take an airplane trip. Arrange the classroom chairs to resemble airplane seats. Make luggage using the file folder storage idea on page 14.

Talking enhances language. Use these open-ended questions during this activity:

- Where is the plane going, and how long will it take?
- What kind of snacks should we eat?
- What should we do once we get there?

## Teaching Tips

Make many of the books you used throughout the year available for free-time browsing. Ask the children to retell the story by looking at the pictures.

Help the children discover the opposites *float* and *sink* by experimenting with a dishpan full of water to see what types of things will float. Try wood, rocks, plastic things, paper clips, etc. Have the children explore wet and dry sand and other objects that are wet or dry. Ask children to recognize other opposites around the play yard (soft/hard, etc.).

## Art Activity

Fish printing is a wonderful, but smelly activity to do with young children. Purchase a large fish from the local fish market or butcher shop. (Often, shopkeepers will donate the fish if they know it is for a school.) Have children take turns painting the fish and then laying it down on a large piece of white paper, gently patting it to make the imprint. As each child completes his or her print, invite him or her to sprinkle glitter lightly over the paint to simulate the sparkle of fish scales. Talk about the different parts of the fish as the activity progresses. Keep a large bucket or pan of clean water handy to rinse the fish between artists.

## Supporting Children with Special Needs

Support fine motor skills by having the children use the pincer grasp to glue round cereal pieces onto an octopus or shells onto sand paper. Enhance gross motor skills by engaging in water play with wind-up fish toys in the water table. Or go fishing with a wooden dowel pole, paper fish, paper clips, and a magnet on the fishing line.

## Enrichment

Share the following rhyme and ask the children to create some rhymes of their own.

I like to fish and boating is such fun,
I like to dig and play in the warm summer sun.
I like to swim and when I am done,
I am so happy that summer has begun.

## Book Suggestion

Carle, Eric. *The Very Clumsy Click Beetle.* Philomel Books, 1999.

# Meeting the Standards: Summer Unit

## Language Arts

- Listens
- Demonstrates competency in speaking as a tool for learning
- Demonstrates competency in listening as a tool for learning
- Is developing fine motor skills
- Produces meaningful linguistic sounds
- Responds to oral directions
- Responds to oral questions
- Uses picture clues to aid comprehension
- Uses picture clues to make predictions about content

## Mathematics

- Estimates quantities
- Explores activities involving chance
- Identifies equal/unequal portions
- Implements a problem-solving strategy
- Uses verbal communication
- Uses pictorial communication
- Uses symbolic communication

## Science

- Applies problem-solving skills
- Classifies
- Communicates
- Discusses changes in seasons
- Explores insects
- Explores fish
- Explores animals
- Identifies color in the real world
- Observes, identifies, and measures objects
- Predicts
- Problem solves through group activities
- Recognizes opposites (soft/hard)

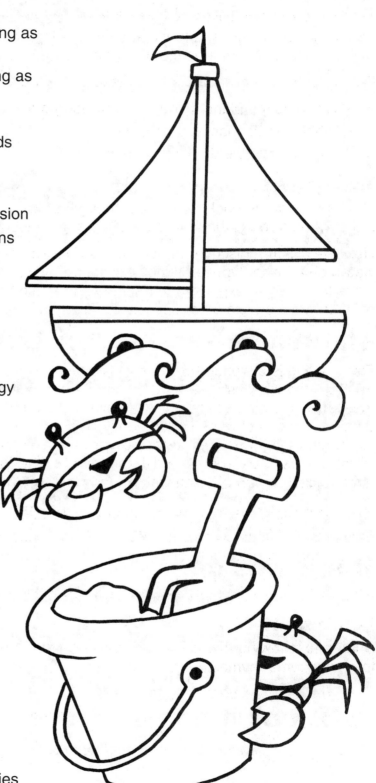

# Five Little Seashells

**Five little seashells lying on the shore.**

*(Place five seashells on the flannelboard.)*

**Swish went the waves and then there were four.**

*(Take one seashell off the flannelboard.)*

**Four little seashells cozy as can be.**

**Swish went the waves and then there were three.**

*(Take one seashell off the flannelboard.)*

**Three little seashells all pearly new.**

**Swish went the waves and then there were two.**

*(Take one seashell off the flannelboard.)*

**Two little seashells sleeping in the sun.**

**Swish went the waves and then there was one.**

*(Take one seashell off the flannelboard.)*

**One little seashell left all alone**

**Whispered, "Shhhhhhh,"**

**as I took it home.**

*(Take the final seashell off the flannelboard.)*

• • • • • • • • • • • • • • • • • • • • • • • • • • • • • • • • • • • • • • • • • • • • • • • • • • • • •

Use the patterns on page 91 to create five seashell flannel pieces.

• • • • • • • • • • • • • • • • • • • • • • • • • • • • • • • • • • • • • • • • • • • • • • • • • • • • •

# Patterns for Five Little Seashells

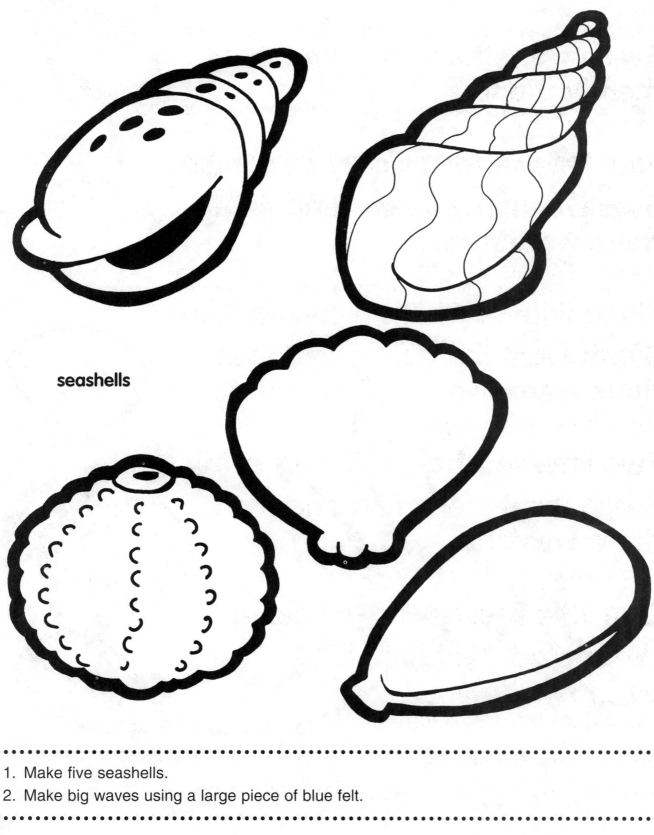

seashells

. . . . . . . . . . . . . . . . . . . . . . . . . . . . . . . . . . . . . . . . . . . . . . . . . . . . . . . . . . . . .

1. Make five seashells.
2. Make big waves using a large piece of blue felt.

. . . . . . . . . . . . . . . . . . . . . . . . . . . . . . . . . . . . . . . . . . . . . . . . . . . . . . . . . . . . .

# Five Little Fish

**Five little fish swam till they were sore.**
*(Put five fish on the flannelboard.)*

**The blue one swam away and then there were four.**
*(Take the blue fish away.)*

**Four little fish went into the big sea.**

**The red one swam away and then there were three.**
*(Take the red fish away.)*

**Three little fish were looking for their friend Mr. Minnow Blue.**
*(Have Mr. Minnow Blue swim quickly by.)*

**The green one swam away and then there were two.**
*(Take the green fish away.)*

**Two little fish were only having fun.**

**The pink one swam away, then there was only one.**
*(Take the pink fish away.)*

**The last little fish just wanted to be a hero.**

**So he swam to save a friend and then there were zero.**
*(Take the final fish away.)*

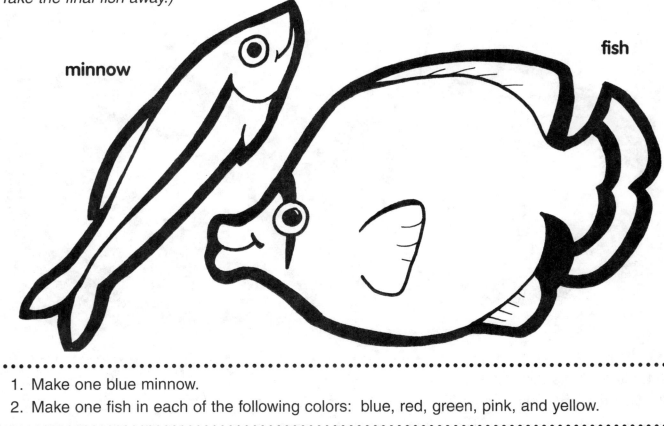

minnow

fish

1. Make one blue minnow.
2. Make one fish in each of the following colors:  blue, red, green, pink, and yellow.

# Summer Vacation

*(Sing to the tune of "She'll Be Coming Round the Mountain.")*

**We're going on vacation in the summer.**
**We're going on vacation in the summer.**
**We'll be packing all our clothes.**
*(Place the suitcases on the flannelboard.)*

**We'll be packing all our clothes.**
**We'll be packing all our clothes for vacation.**

**We'll be driving to the beach in the summer.**
**We'll be driving to the beach in the summer.**
**We'll be putting on our suits,**
*(Place the boy and the girl in swimsuits on the flannelboard.)*

**We'll be putting on our suits,**
**We'll be putting on our suits in the summer.**

**We'll build castles in the sand at the beach.**
*(Place the sand castles on the flannelboard.)*

**We'll build castles in the sand at the beach.**
**We'll be swimming,**
**we'll be splashing.**
*(Place the big waves on the flannelboard.)*

**We'll be swimming,**
**we'll be splashing.**
**We'll be having summer fun**
**at the beach.**

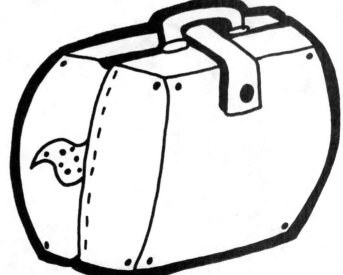

**suitcase**

Use the pattern above for the suitcase. Use the patterns on page 94 to create the boy and girl, and the sand castles.

# Patterns for Summer Vacation

sand castle

girl

boy

..............................................................................

1. Make one boy and girl in swimsuits.
2. Make two sand castles.  One could be enlarged for variation.
3. Make big waves using a large piece of blue felt.
4. Make two different-colored suitcases using the pattern on page 93.

..............................................................................

# Shining Bright

The sun shines bright,
The sun shines bright.
Way up in the summer sky,
The sun shines bright.

The sun fades away,
The sun fades away.
Way down in the horizon,
The sun fades away.

The moon shines bright.
The moon shines bright.
Way up in the summer sky,
The moon shines bright.

The stars twinkle light.
The stars twinkle light.
Way up in the summer sky,
The stars twinkle light.

Use the sun, moon, and stars patterns on page 96.

# Patterns for Shining Bright

sun

moon

stars

**Editor**
Kim Fields

**Editorial Project Manager**
Mara Ellen Guckian

**Editor-in-Chief**
Sharon Coan, M.S. Ed.

**Illustrators**
Alexandra Artigas
Kevin Barnes

**Cover Artist**
Brenda DiAntonis

**Photography**
Lesley Palmer

**Art Coordinator**
Kevin Barnes

**Art Director**
CJae Froshay

**Imaging**
James Edward Grace
Rosa C. See

**Product Manager**
Phil Garcia

**Publishers**
Rachelle Cracchiolo, M.S. Ed.
Mary Dupuy Smith, M.S. Ed.

# Puppet & Flannelboard Stories for Seasons and Holidays

## Authors

*Belinda Dunnick Karge, Ph.D. and
Marian Meta Dunnick, M.S.*

***Teacher Created Materials, Inc.***
6421 Industry Way
Westminster, CA 92683
www.teachercreated.com
**ISBN-0-7439-3700-7**
©2003 Teacher Created Materials, Inc.
Made in U.S.A.

# Table of Contents